WHAT OTHER PEOPLE ARE SAYING ABOUT *1*

Nothing is more exciting than to find the "good works" God has assigned us to do. Marc, Frank and Don have outlined a simple, motivating process to focus your life, find your good works—and then go for it.

— Paul Stanley, former executive vice president of The Navigators

---

"This book will not let you stay on the sidelines. It will challenge you and equip you to find your place in the story that God is writing in our world. I love the practical approach and pastoral feel to this well-written book."

— Brady Boyd, Pastor of New Life Church, Author of *Fear No Evil*

"If you want to be fully alive; If you long to discover how your gifts, talents, and skills come together into a convergence of deep joy; if you realize that this life is more about significance than security; if you are a person who asks the deeper questions of why God put you on this earth—then this book is for you! Appropriately named The 2:10 *Project because Ephesians 2:10 says that you are a "poem" of God, this book has helped me to discover again how to walk in the poem God has written in my heart. Read, meditate, listen to God, do the online projects, and let the Divine Poet write His poem through you."*

— Steve Holt, Founder and Lead Pastor, Mountain Springs Church Founder of Word & Spirit Network

"As an Academic Dean of a Bible college, I frequently run into people who are trying to discern God's will for their lives. The 2:10 Project will be very helpful for anyone looking to identify God's unique plan and purpose."

— Joseph Parle, Ph.D., Academic Dean of the College of Biblical Studies of Houston, Texas

— —

The universal question in every human heart is "who am I" and "what am I to do." These questions — inescapable. The answers — elusive, if you don't know where and how to look. This book will help give you the eyes to see who you are and what you are here to do - your calling. Marc and I have walked together for many years, so I know he is a man who "sees." Treat this book as a treasure map to your calling. It will help get you there.

— Gary Barkalow, Author of *It's Your Call: What Are You Doing Here?*, Founder of The Noble Heart.

210⚘PROJECT

*Discover Your Place
In God's Story*

MARC FEY, DON ANKENBRANDT, AND FRANK JOHNSON

ALLIANCE PUBLISHING GROUP

COPYRIGHT INFORMATION

2:10 Project: Discover Your Place in God's Story

First Printing, 2011

ISBN: 978-0-9836814-0-3

Printed in the United States of America

Cover Design by Third Floor Media, Inc.

Interior Design by Vic Wheeler

DEDICATIONS

Marc

— — — — — — — — — —

To my wife Kathy and our children, Jonathan, Paul and
Annie—your collective candor, wit, and wisdom have made the
pursuit of my own calling, as well as the writing of this book,
possible—and worth it.

Don

— — — — — — — — — —

To my wife Susie and our children D.J., Jamie and Jake. Following
the Lord's path for each of us is such an amazing adventure. I love
you and am proud of how God is using you in His awesome plan.

Frank

— — — — — — — — — —

To my best friend and wife Cindy—your amazing courage, calling
and faith have inspired me as we've journeyed this Kingdom
adventure together. I love you.

ACKNOWLEDGEMENTS

Marc Fey: I want to thank my wife and soul mate Kathy, whose love for me and our kids has helped to make these first 25 years an amazing adventure. To my children, Jonathan, Paul, and Annie, who inspire and challenge me in ways they'll never know.

Thanks to my "Band of Brothers," — Gary Barkalow, David Bervig, and Brad Beck, who have championed God's glory in and through my life. I thank my co-authors, Frank and Don, with whom it has been a privilege and joy to be on mission together at this time in our lives.

I am indebted to God-sent mentors whose friendship and investment in me has helped to shape the message of *The 2:10 Project*: Dr. Del Tackett, Dr. Michael Clifford, Paul Stanley, and my close friend Phil Mathis, whom I miss greatly since his passing in the fall of 2009.

Friends have provided timely encouragement and valuable input along the way: Thomas Smiley, Brad Wright, Glenn Stanton, Joe Rispoli, Matthew Ayers, Luke Brasel, Kathy DeMattee, Barbara Freeman, Steve Maegdlin, Seth Grotelueschen, Brad Miller, Brady Boyd, Steve Holt, Gordon Pennington, Richard Kaiser, Larry Schwarz, Ken Gire, Dr. Mike Bird, Daniel Weiss, Vince D'Acchioli, Chuck Bentley, and Sean Harvey. I am grateful for the support of my family: mom, Connie Fey, dad, Les Fey, and sisters, Lisa Seaton and Nicole Miller.

Finally, I thank my Lord and Savior, Jesus Christ, whose gracious invitation into the Story of all stories has captured me — for eternity. The message of *The 2:10 Project* is the day-to-day pursuit to live in this Story. Every good result from *The 2:10 Project* belongs wholly to Jesus Christ.

Don Ankenbrandt: First and foremost to my Lord Jesus Christ, who has freed me, protected me, given me purpose and joy in His assignments that He has prepared for me…and my longing to be with Him for all of eternity…it does not get any better than this.

I wish to thank the men who have mentored me over my 30-plus years of following Jesus, who have had such a tremendous impact on my life: Ralph Keel who led me to Christ and has been my guide for all of my Christian life; Steve Franklin who was there when I was in my darkest days of being called and who helped me learn to trust the Lord with radical abandon; Tom Wilson who I have had the privilege of working under in two kingdom assignments…Young Life and Halftime; and Bob Buford whose book *Halftime* redirected my entire life toward what matters most…things that impact eternity. I am grateful beyond words to you men that God has used so mightily.

To Mike and Sandy Whitten, and Charles and Mary White: you have been such a huge source of encouragement and support to Susie and me…thank you does not say enough…Rock and Roll!! Most importantly, to my wife Susie who in my opinion is the most amazing person on this earth. I love you and can't believe the Lord let me find you.

Frank Johnson: I remain amazed by the grace of my Lord and Savior Jesus Christ. As the plan for my life continues to unfold, I am humbled and grateful for the opportunity to serve His Kingdom.

As a proud father, thanks to my three children Ryan, Troy and Jessica. Ryan and Troy—you remind me every day how a new generation of believers is rising up to re-capture ground lost to a turbulent culture. My beautiful daughter Jessica—your courage, strength, and perseverance has been a blessing to those who know your incredible story.

I am indebted to my grandfather, friend, pastor and namesake—the late Reverend Frank E. Nies who helped me discover and construct a solid foundation of faith that I carry with me every day of my life. My memories of his words and wisdom will never be forgotten.

Thanks to my co-authors and contributors Marc, Don, Tim and Rodney. What a privilege to be on this mission with each of you, my brothers.

It was a sincere honor for me to be part of the Community Impact Outreach team that served so many hurting communities. Thank you Chris, Mike, Cory, Don, Jeff, Julie, Kathy, Cosa, Linda, Gary Allen, Melissa and, of course, Janet (our "glue")—certainly God used your collective hard work, dedication and passion for His glory.

Finally, blessings and thanks to so many Christ-followers we've met across the country who have discovered their unique place in God's story. The difference you make in your families, churches and cities is changing the world.

TABLE OF CONTENTS

FOREWORD

The most important thing any object within the universe can engage in is the ultimate purpose for which it was created. It not only results in great practical consequences, but it brings great pleasure and glory to its creator. Nothing delights the master craftsman more than to hear his violin in the hands of the virtuoso; nothing would pain him more than to see it beating dust from a rug.

So, too, is our Creator delighted to see the work of His hands skillfully performing the functions for which He made them. The atoms do this well. So does the complex machinery within the living cell. For me, nothing matches the beauty of a horse when it is running. Horses are made to run. All of God's creation carries out the tasks for which they were crafted. All, that is, except the human. We will never see the horse trying to write novels or the zebra attempting to make shoes.

But humans? Well, they are very complex. They can do many different things, and they have a lot of motivations that can sway them in deciding which thing to do—motives such as money, prominence, parental pressure, the easiest path, that which is "cool" or in fashion or makes me think better of myself or makes me think others will think better of myself, etc. and etc. It is for this reason that we have men filling pulpits who should be teaching biology at the university or planting corn or drilling for oil. Conversely, we have those who are designing software who should be standing in the pulpit.

But even more so, we have the large part of the Body of Christ who have missed their awesome calling to be the good neighbor, to minister to others. We have somehow bought the false notion that the state or the church or some Ministry should be doing these things. But in so doing, we have neglected one of the prime means, our good works, by which the world around us would glorify our

Father. Instead, the world glorifies the state. This should not be.

I work constantly with university students, and by far the single greatest question they have is: what is my role in life? I always tell them that I will answer their question on the last day. My answer, "I have no clue. But I know the One Who does. I know the One Who made you and crafted you and placed within you His gifts and talents and has fashioned you for a delightful purpose. And, He will not make you for a divine purpose and then hide it from you."

This is the purpose of this book. It is to help you, guide you, cheer you on in your quest to find the divine purpose for your life—all of life. One thing you will not find in these pages, thankfully, is the notion that to serve God you must be in "full-time" Christian ministry. In fact, you may be surprised to discover that your vocation, whether that is driving a truck or being a plumber, will be held in high esteem. If this is what God has made you for, then there is no higher or divine calling.

But the social order God has designed for us includes more than our vocation. We are called to be a loving husband or wife. We are called to a true fellowship with believers. We are called into a personal relationship with God. We are called to be good citizens. And, we are all called to "minister" to others.

All of this requires a balanced life, but it also requires an understanding of what God has made us for. Much of what follows will focus on helping you examine that design in your life—your passions and hunger, what makes your heart sing and what makes it weep, what lights you up, what energizes you. These and many other practical guides are laid out here to aid you in that grand quest.

The Lord has greatly blessed *The Truth Project* and He has worked deeply in millions of lives. But one of my greatest regrets was that we didn't provide the follow-up for people who ended the study with the question: "What do I do now?" I am thankful that Marc and Frank and Don have taken the time to provide an easy-to-follow process for people to begin to answer that question.

May the Lord bless this effort and you personally as you seek to join the grand adventure in which God has called each of us to participate.

Soli Deo Gloria!

Dr. Del Tackett

Section 1: **Identity**

When you believe and embrace who God is and who He has created you to be, then your calling, purpose, and life mission work themselves out.

1

QUICK START
WHAT YOU NEED TO KNOW
ABOUT THIS BOOK

"The place God calls you is where your deep gladness and the world's hunger meet."

— Frederick Buechner

"So, why are you here?" Don* asked a group of men and women who gathered to go through *The 2:10 Project*. Their answers confirmed for us what we've discovered over the last five years: People are looking for their place in God's story.

One man, a commercial real estate developer, answered, "The economic downturn has been hard. But now I'm looking for a different kind of success, other than just making money."

A woman, whose now quiet "empty nest" gave her more time than she'd had in 25 years, said, "I'm involved in six different things right now, and I want to find one or two that really tap into who I am and what I've experienced in my life. I'm hoping to get some clarity."

A young professional man explained, "I'm in my 30s, with young kids at home, a good marriage, and a job I care about. But I don't want to be like my parents, who waited until they retired to start doing significant things in life. I want to find my life mission now so I have a whole lifetime to pursue it."

Another woman quietly said, "Since my divorce two years ago, I've taken a lot of time to look at my life. My kids are almost grown, and even though I'm still hurting over my divorce, I feel like God has something important for me to do. I want to find what that is."

QUESTIONS AND ANSWERS

This book answers two questions:

1. "Why am I here?"
2. "What does God *really* want me to do with my life?"

In fact, the answers come from one simple but powerful 22-word verse that also provides the book's title: Ephesians 2:10. This verse says, "For we are his workmanship, created in Christ Jesus for good

---

* Three of us contributed to this book, but Marc is the "voice" as the author; with Don and Frank referred to by name, and at times, quoted at length.

works, which God prepared beforehand that we should walk in them"
(NKJV). The answers to these two questions define your place in
God's grand story and help you discover your unique spiritual DNA.

As we begin this journey together, let me explain a few important
truths about this powerful verse.

Ephesians 2:10 is what I would call a design verse.[1] Passages in the
Bible can be descriptive or prescriptive: Descriptive means telling us
how things are or should be, while prescriptive means telling us what
to do or not do. Ephesians 2:10 isn't a prescription for life, telling us
to go be the workmanship of God or that we need to go find those
good works that God has prepared in advance for us to do.

Rather, this verse states a truth. It describes God's wonderful
design for our lives, worked out through His redemptive plan: "You
are God's workmanship." Statement of fact. Reality. A truth you can
count on.

God also tells us what we were made for: "Created in Christ Jesus
for good works." Statement of fact. Reality. A truth you can count on.

And He tells us that He has done His part, setting up the way for
us to be successful in doing these works: "Good works, which *God
prepared* beforehand." Yes, you get it—statement of fact. Reality. A
truth you can count on.

Just one part of this whole verse is conditional, and we find the
condition in the final six words: *"that we should walk in them."*
Through these six words, God invites us to set our course in a certain
direction, to *walk* in a certain way.

This book is all about helping you believe the reality of God's
truth found in the first 16 words and helping you know how to take
action on His invitation found in the last six words.

A POINT OF REFERENCE

When I worked at Focus on the Family a few years ago, I helped produce *The Truth Project*, a video-based, 12-part biblical worldview

study.[2] If you've been through a *Truth Project* small group, you'll remember the end of the last DVD. Dr. Del Tackett, the teacher and creator of the study, raises a simple but powerful question that many of his students ask him: *"What do I do?"* On the screen behind Del the following words appear: "I have no clue." However, Del then says a very encouraging thing: "But I know the One who does."

This book will help you through a process Del points to — to hear from the One who does know what you were created for. In fact, God invites you to join Him on this journey to discover the answer to that question. That's why we describe this process as "more than reading a book;" it's a set of directions to help you get moving. Accordingly, you'll find online assessments and other activities to make this discussion *highly* practical. You'll find more about the online sections at the end of this chapter.

If you've been a believer in Jesus for any length of time, you know — at least intellectually — that God made you for a purpose. In addition, you realize that God gives you tasks to do, some short in duration, others lasting years, which we call "assignments," that connect to your purpose and calling. In the pages ahead, we'll guide you through activities that make you aware of God's assignments in your life. For one purpose: To help you find your answer to Del's question: "What do I do?" We'll point you to God, to the One Who does know what we are to do.

> **If you've been a believer in Jesus for any length of time, you know — at least intellectually — that God made you for a purpose.**

Most importantly, understand that we'll walk you through a very intentional process. Along the way, we'll help you consider other important and related questions — deeper questions that reach way down into our hearts and touch the very essence of who we are. These are questions such as:

- "Why am I here?"
- "What if I don't have what it takes to fulfill my calling?"
- "Have my life mistakes disqualified me?"
- "Will the daily struggles I experience keep me from finding my life mission?"
- "Is it possible I've wasted too much time to find my calling—is it too late for me?"

In addition, we'll help you answer these questions against the backdrop of our culture—one that isn't particularly conducive to finding your God assignments. Our culture is likely to answer the questions a different way than God does, such as:

- "You can't do it."
- "What's the point?"
- "You tried that, and it didn't work out."
- "Others are more gifted and 'called' than you are."
- "You are way too busy to add another thing to your life."

So our culture says.

In the pages that follow, we will introduce you to people who have found the answer to the question, "What is my assignment, Lord?" Although we use Ephesians 2:10 as the basis for finding your assignment, you'll see that God doesn't offer a one-size-fits-all approach. Instead, just as each person's story is unique, so is each person's process. Through the process, we pray you'll discover (or rediscover) a vibrant relationship with God, the One who absolutely knows what He has made you for.

INTRODUCTIONS: AN EXPRESSION OF GOD'S WORK IN US

Before we dive in, let us introduce ourselves. I am Marc Fey, and my friends are Don Ankenbrandt and Frank Johnson. We'll serve as your coaches and fellow travelers through the process of discovering your calling and life mission. We'll take you to communities around the United States and introduce you to truly heroic people we know. These are regular people who found their assignments from God and who are living them out in compelling and inspirational ways. Also, because Don, Frank, and I are friends and colleagues in this great adventure, we hope you'll see the importance of walking out your own process with others.

Although I'm doing the writing, this book is very much a collaborative effort by all three of us. In fact, the notion of calling is all about *belonging*—to God and to one another. We call this the context of "community." While new technologies in the past decade or so have dramatically changed the way we think of community, it remains true that our calling is expressed in the context of relationships. Even though calling is intensely private, it is also always very public. As you begin to understand your calling in the context of meaningful relationships, you'll be able to articulate your life's mission—the practical pathway of your calling—and how that works best with friends and others who have input into your life, just as Don, Frank and I have all had in each other's lives.

In addition, calling is about time and place. We all have the need for a sense of being rooted in our lives. We desire a place to grow, where we can build strong relationships with the people around us, and where over time we experience a shared history together. All Kingdom impact happens among certain people, in certain places, at certain times, and this history is the work of a Sovereign God who is intimately involved in the details of our lives. These essential ingredients of story are incredibly important to finding and fulfilling our individual and collective callings in Christ.

Put a different way, my calling has no context apart from the community where I work and the neighborhood where I live. Neither does yours. We're all inextricably linked to one another. And if we want to understand our calling so we can articulate our life's mission, we must also understand the communities where we live as well as the communities where we're called to go.

Our calling is also connected to the unique, perplexing, and complicated challenges of our day. These challenges find expression in our culture — the ads, products, services, art, music, trends in technologies, and myriad of other culture-producing "things." These challenges also manifest themselves in various social spheres — government at all levels, schools, churches, and businesses.

Our calling is also one of wonder and mystery. We want you to see that *you* are that wonder, and *your life in God* is that mystery. The Living God extends a deeply personal and absolutely unique call to each of us. He invites us to find our calling, and He generously offers us the opportunity to experience a deep joy when we engage our place in His story of redemption. I've found truth in Frederick Buechner's poignant observation: "The place God calls you is where your deep gladness and the world's hunger meet."[3]

He invites us to find our calling, and He generously offers us the opportunity to experience a deep joy when we engage our place in His story of redemption.

You will get to know Don, Frank, and I pretty well as we talk about calling and life mission. Sometimes, you'll see us in ways that will make us feel uncomfortable or embarrassed, because we'll share not just a long series of successes but also a few missteps and misfires. In other words, we want you to know that discovering your own calling might get a little messy at times! However, this is where we most often find the fingerprints of God — in the messiness of human activity.

As we work through *The 2:10 Project*, and as you discern your passions and clarify your giftings and learn from our experiences and your own, we hope you'll realize we are traveling on this journey with you. Our prayer and expectation is that you absolutely will find your place in God's story — your "calling," along with your specific

Kingdom assignments.

Be prepared for an exciting and unpredictable road ahead!

A MODEL OF TRANSFORMATION

A word or two about our learning approach. The concepts and truths presented in *The 2:10 Project*, the questions we ask, and the activities we recommend reflect our "model for transformation." Essentially, we believe that most of us don't need more information; instead we need a fresh encounter with God and His truth. God gives us insight through intentional activities—tasks that help us reflect on the past, present, and future that serve as data input about our calling. And, we are certain that life-changing transformation occurs in the context of relationships. We build on the belief that God is the One who empowers us for change. We illustrate the transformation model as follows:

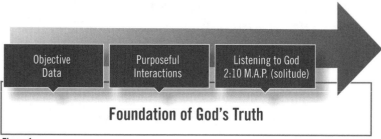

Figure 1

The process begins with objective inputs. These "data points" help us evaluate our lives against God's Word. In this book and its online experience, practical inputs along the way will help you see whether or not you actually live out what you claim to believe about God's truth.

In addition, true learning occurs through meaningful interactions—with God and with others. So, we've provided opportunities for meaningful interactions.[4] The goal of these online interactions is to really drive home the transformational change God desires for you.

You'll also see two "take aways" at the end of this book. The first is instruction on how to do a day of solitude. The second is a personalized "Mission Action Plan"—what we call the 2:10 M.A.P.. This is a practical and intentional strategy for finding your personal life mission.

Finally, the foundation of the entire process is God's truth. Romans 12:2 challenges us to be transformed by the renewing of our minds so we can discern God's perfect will for our lives. The living truth of God's Word provides the foundation we build on. Using this foundation, we learn to see the world according to *reality,* God's truth.

A PERSONAL INVESTMENT

To make the most of your investment in *The 2:10 Project,* you need to interact with the material. Even better, share what you're learning with others who know you and care about your journey with God.

As you begin the process, choose the amount of time and effort you want. The activities provide what you will need for the 2:10 M.A.P., including instructions and support materials for your day of solitude. If you're very busy or swamped with other life challenges, be sure to at least complete the assessments, providing you with insight into your unique spiritual DNA. This will give you great tools to take action.

The activities also present you with the opportunity to take a much deeper dive and will include email interactions, online opportunities for real-time learning, and invitations to participate with others through your learning experience. Whatever the amount of time you have to give, you'll log on to interact with the materials. More importantly, you'll be inviting us to serve as your coaches. We'll use the results we gather from online interactions to challenge you in areas for growth in your life.

We've participated in the process we will lay out for you. We've also used it to help many people find their calling and life mission *and* apply it to their spheres of influence. In *The 2:10 Project,* we've designed personal and group activities, all pointing to one objective:

We want you to *own* this process. You'll want to engage in the simple act of self-expression, prompted by the exercises we give you, to help you understand your own journey. If you can do that with others, all the better.

In fact, you'll realize that *The 2:10 Project* is a great book to read with others, perhaps in a small group study or during weekly meetings at a coffee shop. Both our experience and research show that deeper learning happens when we experience it with others — in community. In fact, we regularly hear how *2:10 Project* groups continue to meet long after the study is over, as group members become coaches in each other's lives.

The former English teacher in me knows how the telling of our stories often changes us. Expressing ourselves through story can help us master what we're learning, and that expression leads to personal discovery at least as much as any intellectual discovery of God's truth. Let His Word search you. Own it. Courageously pursue it. Of course, we all must do our own work — I can't do the work for you any more than you can do it for me. But the pastor in me wholeheartedly cheers you along in the process!

Let His Word search you. Own it. Courageously pursue it.

Don, Frank, and I have learned from our own experiences, as well as from walking with others, that you will already know the answers to many of the questions we'll be asking. So, we agree with what author Oswald Chambers noted: "The author who benefits you most is not the one who tells you something you did not know before, but the one who gives expression to the truth that has been dumbly struggling in you for utterance."[5] Chambers' statement summarizes why this book is about helping you find your place, one that God invites you to join Him in. I firmly believe that we will find God in these deep conversations, since He is the one who knows us deeply — the only One, truly.

A NEW ASSIGNMENT

I was in the middle of my 35th *Truth Project* training conference. Over a three-year period, I'd been working with Del Tackett and leading the team delivering this transformational conference all over the United States and to a few countries internationally. This particular session was at a church on the outskirts of Birmingham, Alabama—a quaint, white-pillared brick building, with bright sunlight angling into the auditorium as I spoke from the front. Then, right there in the middle of leading one of the sessions, I knew what the Lord was telling me. Deep in my heart, I sensed Him saying, "It's time to go 'do' *The Truth Project*." My understanding of this whisper of the Lord's leading grew in the weeks that followed. But even in *that* moment, I knew I was on a "new assignment" from the Lord. This new assignment was a part of the larger mission of my life, and it changed my world—again.

The Lord has a way of doing that in our lives, doesn't He? I'll share more about this assignment in the pages that follow, as well as Don's and Frank's stories of God's calling in their lives. But sharing the story here illustrates something important: Discussions of calling and life purpose don't take place on our terms, but God's. Anticipate all you want, but I promise you will not be able to predict where this process leads.

With that in mind, remember that the first steps of reflection can often be difficult. We all have disappointments in what hasn't yet come to pass, as well as discouragement in things we've tried to do, but failed. Sometimes we must face the reality that the expression of our faith has been mediocre, even uninspired. One of Don's favorite quotes challenges us to get past these roadblocks: "Your faith will either become a boring habit or an acute fever."[6] Which one describes you?

If you believe you were created to do something specific and life-changing—that your life is destined to have eternal impact—this book is for you. If you want to find your Kingdom assignment but don't exactly know where to go, this book is for you. If religious activities like attending church services, Bible study, serving in the children's ministry, faithfully writing tithe checks—as important as they might be—are no longer enough for you in your walk with God, this book is for you.

Perhaps you already have a rich history of fruitful ministry—you've found your calling—but you sense that God is leading you to a new place. Maybe you sense that we are living in times that will require a different kind of contribution from Christians, a new understanding of calling. *The 2:10 Project* will help you find that new Kingdom assignment by helping you understand your unique spiritual DNA. And if I might hazard a guess, I think you will find your calling is much bigger than you can imagine.

Dig in to the experience

When you purchased *The 2:10 Project,* you purchased more than a book. Your purchase includes access to the complete set of online interactions that will guide you through the process to create your unique 2:10 M.A.P. - your Ministry Action Plan.

If you ordered *The 2:10 Project* online, you should have received your login credentials via email. If you purchased the book from a retailer or at a 2:10 Conference, you would have received an insert card in the front of the book with your login credentials.

Log on now at **www.210project.com** to access the online interactive assessments and exercises.

2

STORY
CALLING INTERSECTS WITH COMMUNITY AND CULTURE

"God did not direct His call to Isaiah—Isaiah overheard God saying, '…who will go for Us?' The call of God is not just for a select few but for everyone. Whether I hear God's call or not depends on the condition of my ears, and exactly what I hear depends upon my spiritual attitude."

—Oswald Chambers

Don calls Lorenzo Brown "Jesus in a wheelchair." Lorenzo reflects Jesus—His character, His heart, His values. As you might have guessed, Lorenzo spends most of his day in a wheelchair.

Lorenzo has come a long way from where he used to be. At the age of 17, Lorenzo got into a fight over a baseball cap. Growing up on the streets of a poor community in rural Alabama, Lorenzo's life changed dramatically in just a few hours.

Following a retaliatory drive-by shooting—in the flash of a moment and a gun barrel—Lorenzo lay on the ground bleeding. In the hours ahead he would learn that he was a quadraplegic, never able to move most of his body again. The story gets worse from there. Because his family was unable to care for him, Lorenzo moved to a nursing home. For two years, he didn't receive a single visitor. One day, a girl—a teenager about Lorenzo's age—showed up in his room. In the days and weeks ahead, she came by more and more frequently, and their friendship grew. Over time, she read the Bible to Lorenzo. Eventually, Lorenzo met Jesus.

Let's stop there for just a moment. Do you see the wonderful and miraculous story here? A teenage girl. A series of simple times talking. Two people who seemed to have nothing in common. A friendship. A young man's hardened heart softening to the love of God. Two stories of calling taking place—both the girl's and Lorenzo's. God born in a manger, crucified, risen…this Living God present with a young girl and a deeply wounded young man.

The rest of the story. Through some very complicated circumstances, Lorenzo next ended up in a rehabilitation center, where he met David who was also paralyzed. After years of sitting and lying around, despondence gripped Lorenzo and David. Their depression led them to the same anguishing conclusion: "We need to commit suicide so we can go be with the Lord." "What good are we here just sitting around?" They quickly wondered, "But how should we do it?

We can't shoot ourselves because we can't hold a gun. We can't poison ourselves, because we can't drive a car to go buy the poison." Imagine the desperation you'd feel knowing you have no capacity to do anything for yourself, not even end your own life.

One day, while riding outside in their wheelchairs, they drove past the pool. They'd figured out a way to die; they would run their wheelchairs into the pool and drown. With their plan in place, they readied themselves and headed out. Yet just as they were moving toward the plunge, it hit Lorenzo, *Why did God allow this to happen to us? Certainly, He must have a reason.* In fact, Lorenzo had already thought about talking to David about not killing themselves, because God had been speaking

Why did God allow this to happen to us? Certainly, He must have a reason.

to him. He sensed the Lord saying to him, "Take the D out of Disabled, and what do you get? Is-able." God's intimate conversation with Lorenzo was changing his life. There, within sight of the pool that would have ushered them home to be with Jesus, God revealed His plan for them—start a ministry to encourage and help people with catastrophic disabilities learn how to live on their own.

Lorenzo did just that. He started Is-Able Ministries, speaking at prisons and talking to at-risk kids about how their behavior has consequences, as his did. He teaches the Word and shares his story. He lives without disability funding, Medicare, or governmental help. He gets around town in his custom-equipped van, that he drives himself. In fact, Don loves to talk about how amazing it is to ride in Lorenzo's van, "I can't believe I'm riding around town in a van driven by a man who can only partially move his arms. Yes, no doubt God has made you Is-Able!"

Four years ago, God gave Lorenzo an amazing wife, April, and they now have twin boys. And to me, like many others in his town who have witnessed the miracle of his life, Lorenzo is more like Jesus than any person we've met. His vision is to one day open up the "Is-Able Center," to help people trapped by disability become able and independent, helping others discover the truth that set him free — they have a purpose and God can use them in ways they could never expect.

Lorenzo's story is amazing, isn't it? So is yours! Two things occur when God calls his people to action: the ministry *through* an individual and the ministry *in* that individual. Besides the ministry of Is-Able *through* Lorenzo's life, the wonderful and mysterious story of God's is at work *in* Lorenzo's life. I love what Oswald Chambers says about this mystery:

> *God brings me into the proper relationship with Himself so that I can understand His call, and then I serve Him on my own out of a motivation of absolute love. Service to God is the deliberate love-gift of a nature that has heard the call of God. Service is an expression of my nature, and God's call is an expression of His nature. Therefore, when I receive His nature and hear His call, His divine voice resounds throughout His nature and mine and the two become one in service. The Son of God reveals Himself in me, and out of devotion to Him service becomes my everyday way of life.[7]*

When we discover our God-given passion and mission, and then develop clarity about how God has uniquely wired us and equipped us with spiritual gifts, passions, and the unique experiences in life, we become infectious to the people around us, affecting others in surprising ways. Often that happens in ways we might never know in this life.

Lorenzo would tell you that this journey to his life mission has changed everything. He is now a man fully committed and resolved to give his life to this God-led journey. He is a man fully alive.

Life mission. Played out in the story of our lives. Changing the communities where we live. A deeply personal call, and no doubt, a public one as well. God's story wrapped up in the details of your life and mine.

When God's calling on a person's life intersects with the deep need in an individual or group of people's lives, God's Kingdom is expressed in powerful ways. Three stories are told when that happens: an individual's personal story (because we're all working out our own journey with God), a community's story (because we're all connected to one another by formal and informal relationships), and God's redemptive story (because we're all connected in time and to one another by God's eternal plan). Understanding your unique spiritual DNA enables you to intentionally engage your relationship with God and with others to discover your place in God's story.

The intersection of these three stories can be a bit like hearing a parable. You understand at some level, almost intuitively, that the story makes sense. But the interpretation or meaning of the story lies just beyond reach. You begin to think, *I know I was made for something significant, but it's just out of my reach to know exactly what that is.* Or *I know I was created to do what I am doing right now, but it feels like in my life's calling, one of the pieces to the puzzle is missing.*

I know I was made for something significant, but it's just out of my reach to know exactly what that is.

We call this process of discernment "learning to interpret the parable of our lives." Discovering our life mission begins by becoming aware of our personal journey with God—with the story that we find ourselves in including situations that have been sources of great pain, as well as times of great joy and abundant life. Like Lorenzo's experience illustrates, we can mine our personal narratives in order to understand the parable of our lives.

SPINNING OUT OF CONTROL

Describing our generation as spinning out of control isn't much of a reach. By "generation" we don't mean a particular life stage or age; more accurately, we mean the age we live in, including all the people who make up our world. Most social indicators confirm that families and communities today face more challenges than previous eras. Divorce rates, declining education scores, lower standard of living, the prevalence of drug and alcohol use, climbing numbers of incarcerated men and women, and many other indicators reveal what we already know from the headlines on the evening news: Life is tougher today.

These are the statistics of our generation, but they provide an inadequate picture of the deep challenge and hardship revealed through our own lives. Even the practical challenges we face are relentless in the way they drag us down every day: one more escalating credit card balance, an uncertain future at work, a complacent look from a spouse whose far-off eyes define a new divide in the relationship, defiant kids with sliding grades and questionable friends.

Yet at this point, God's grace turns most adroitly: "It is often our mistakes that get us going on the spiritual journey. Error is turned into pilgrimage," says Alan Jones in *The Soul's Journey*.[8] Those are encouraging words because we all know deep down that God's greatest moments often come at our weakest times.

The parable of our lives and the story of our generation both require some interpretation to discern what actions we need to take. Usually, we don't struggle to interpret the good things that happen in our lives. Instead, we need understanding and insight into the obstacles, the turns in the road, and the fog where we find ourselves. The same holds true regarding the story taking place in our generation. This is an important issue, because in this book we make the bold assertion that your life mission has a context in the generation, the culture, and even the community where God has placed you. So, interpreting the situations and events taking place around us is just as important as understanding what goes on inside us. Yet if you're like I am, it's not hard to become dulled to the tragedy and depth of hardship in our world today.

DIFFERENT WORLDS

About four years ago, I found myself in one of these places, as I wrestled with the overwhelming obstacles for seeing lasting change in families and communities. Yet in the midst of my own struggle, God chose to strengthen my faith one afternoon. Let me explain.

I was staying at a hotel situated right between two contrasting areas of southern California. When I went a mile to the west of my hotel, I found myself in a high-end financial area of Orange County: BMWs, Mercedes-Benzes, Lexuses and other luxury cars testified to the area's tremendous money-generated power and influence. But a mile to the east, I found myself in an area of Santa Ana that the Rockefeller Institute five years earlier had named the city with the highest hardship index.[9] More than 90 gangs, a dense and over-populated urban environment, high numbers of students on the reduced- and free-lunch program, escalating crime, and rampant drug use characterized this area of California.

I felt like I'd been set up—by God Himself! Just a couple of months earlier, I'd traveled to eastern Kentucky to begin to define, build, and roll out a new model of ministry for Focus on the Family's Community Impact division. The timing was good because I'd spent the previous four years working with Dr.

> **I felt like I'd been set up — by God Himself!**

Del Tackett to produce and launch *The Truth Project*. As I mentioned earlier, God had spoken to me in the quiet of my heart that the time was right to "go and do *The Truth Project*." I understood that to mean it was time to apply biblical worldview thinking to community development and other discipling and training opportunities we'd been considering, with the model built on our best understanding of

God's design for community and ministry.

Our first efforts in eastern Kentucky had been very encouraging. In fact, Frank served as a big part of those efforts, and our friendship first took root there. We were partnering with a nonprofit whose mandate was drug enforcement, rehabilitation, and education to counteract the devastating effects prescription drug addictions had caused in this part of the country. The problem was so bad that in three counties, 49 percent of all the children lived in homes with neither a father nor mother.[10] With the family unit faltering in these communities, our role was to provide the education component as well as a strategy for mobilizing the Body of Christ into the toughest areas of the community. We were encouraged by the quick progress. By all counts, it was a great start.

Now, here I was in this complicated place in Orange County, keenly aware of these two very different worlds, each within a few miles of each other: prosperity and poverty, wealth and affliction.

What happened next is hard to describe. In that moment, it suddenly seemed preposterous to accomplish what we wanted to do with our Community Impact program. Absolutely impossible.

Can you remember a time in your life when you felt the flush of embarrassment rush up into your cheeks, along with a little queasiness in your stomach and confusing thoughts in your mind? That describes the exact feeling overwhelming me in this moment. I became aware of how completely crazy this idea was. Could we really bring together leaders from different spheres of the community, including churches, under one banner of change and transformation? Would it be possible to mobilize the Body of Christ to places in the community where the pain was the greatest, setting in motion "micro-movements" (the term we used for these grassroots-designed efforts)? The words *Wow, what was I thinking?* rolled around in my head and heart for three or four very long minutes as I saw how insurmountable the obstacles seemed to me.

But then I heard God ask me a question in the quiet place of my heart. His question shifted everything for me; it was, as we say, a game changer. God asked me this question:

"Marc, do you think I don't have a plan for this generation?"

Pause. Then this thought: *Yes, Lord, of course you have a plan for our generation! And, it doesn't matter what part—big or small, seen or unseen—we have. It's enough that You are calling us to be a part of Your plan.* In that moment, the backdrop of the impossible scene dropped out of the picture and a new one dropped in. This new wonderful, mysterious, backdrop was "the plan of God for our generation."

So, God replaced my dread with a dream, exchanged embarrassment for joy, and transplanted confusion with confidence. And it all had to do with the adventure of discovering "the plan of God for our generation." These are the moments when we are changed, when "a single event can awaken within us a stranger totally unknown to us," when we discover the truth that "to live is to be slowly born."[11]

Could God really change a community? A city? As an InterVarsity college student, I experienced the transforming power of the Gospel as older students and staff discipled me in what it meant to follow Christ. As a high school teacher—my first job out of college—I saw God change the lives of both students and teachers I prayed for and shared with the goodness and grace of God. Over the next seven years as a pastor, I saw God change and transform a congregation. But a whole city? Years ago, I would have said I believed such change was possible. However, truth be told, that answer would come more from "book-learning knowledge," rather than the kind of experiential knowledge the Holy Spirit uses to teach us through life's events. So here I was with this daunting challenge in front of me—and I really believed that God could do this. That He *would* do it.

That's part of my story—the journey that we've been on in the past seven years. In the pages ahead, Frank will share his story about how God met him in this great adventure, taking him from owning numerous IT companies to a ministry role at Focus on the Family and eventually to the work he's engaged in now: a leader in this effort to spark movement after movement in communities around the country.

And Don will tell you his story, from a Young Life staff member early in his marriage to a successful businessman in his early 30s, back to Young Life as a regional director for 13 years, and now coaching leaders to find their calling by raising up numerous city-changing ministries in a growing number of communities around the country. We might say God has been setting all of us up for something very special.

We want to ask you the question: Have you also lived under an unspoken belief that things have gotten too hard in our generation? Like I did, have you implicitly believed the lie that God's power might be able to do a good thing here and there, but "as far as actually changing the course of our generation...well, that doesn't seem likely." Take a moment to ask God right now to open your eyes and your heart to the reality that He has a wonderful plan for our generation—and you are a part of His plan. I promise you, if you do that, He will show you things in the days and months ahead that will describe the truth of 1 Corinthians 2:6, "Eye has not seen, nor ear heard, nor have entered into the heart of man the things which God has prepared for those who love Him." Hold on to your hat!

> **Take a moment to ask God right now to open your eyes and your heart to the reality that He has a wonderful plan for our generation — and you are a part of His plan.**

THREE STORIES WOVEN TOGETHER

As we move forward together, you'll discover your personal mission by weaving together three narratives: your personal story, our generation's story, and God's transcendent story. What do we mean?

The first story, your *personal story*, is where we will tackle the questions of identity, intimacy with God, passion, purpose, spiritual gifting, and context.

As we've said, by *the story of our generation,* we don't mean a particular life stage or the age of a person. Rather, this second story reflects the "age" we live in, including all the people who make up our world.

And finally, the third story, *the transcendent story of God,* works through human history to rescue a people for Himself. This is the story of redemption.

When woven together, our personal story finds its expression in the story of our generation, and what we do will be a part of the transcendent story told at the end of the age. The tapestry becomes a kind of Hebrews 11 narrative, where faith and action meet and we become a part of the history of people who have fulfilled God's calling on our lives.

As the Body of Christ, one of the mistakes we've made is unwittingly separating our lives from the culture we're in, making us irrelevant in many places within our communities and culture. Somehow, we let the world pass us by. In cases where we didn't let the world pass us by, many of us became more like the world than an effective and distinctive contrast as believers. In other words, your calling will connect you to what our culture specifically needs, and this expression of the Kingdom will fit into the dramatic narrative that reaches back to the Garden of Eden when God first set in motion the merciful and wise plan that would lead to the rescue of His people.

AN ANCIENT ILLUSTRATION

I am always curious about people mentioned in the Bible just once as an illustration of a Kingdom reality. One such example involves the sons of Issachar. You might recall a short phrase in 1 Chronicles 12:32 describing these people as "men who understood the times and knew what Israel should do." In essence, these men had insight about the times they lived in, and because of that—and their hearts of resolve and courage to do the right thing—they took action in ways that changed their world. If you look a little closer at this passage, you'll see that this phrase comes in the narrative describing all of the Israelite warriors who joined David, the anointed but not yet seated King of Israel. You'll recall a very paranoid King Saul had sought David's life.

The first two verses of 1 Chronicles 12 read as follows:

These were the men who came to David at Ziklag, while he was banished from the presence of Saul son of Kish (they were among the warriors who helped him in battle; they were armed with bows and were able to shoot arrows or to sling stones right-handed or left-handed).

A few interesting observations. These gifted and able leaders were multi-talented (shooting arrows and slinging stones left- or right-handed), and they were willing to risk their position and influence formerly held under Saul (they surrendered their official position in Saul's army; as his relatives, they also gave up the favor they received from being associated with him). In other words, *these were trained and mature leaders.*

As the passage goes on, we learn more about this group of fierce and courageous warriors:

- They were "able to handle the shield and spear" (verse 8)
- They had "faces like lions and as were swift as gazelles" (verse 8);

- They were "a match for a hundred, and the greatest for a thousand" (verse 14).
- They had first crossed the Jordan to take on the "giants in the land" (verse 15).

When we get to verse 32, we read: "from Issachar, men who understood the times and knew what Israel should do — 200 chiefs, with all their relatives under their command." Did you catch that? These leaders were leading their families, too. I think this is a strong message for us — God desires for us to be leaders who lead our families and do so with a deep understanding of the times we live in. We are wise. We are insightful. We are creative, imaginative, adaptive, and forward-thinking in how we do ministry. This is the story of our generation. These are leaders who are shrewd — which means they have "practical intelligence." And they are strategic — they "plan to win a battle."

I know you might be thinking, "Yes, I know some people who are 'sons of Issachar.' Gifted leaders. Called. But that's not me." In the chapters ahead, we'll unpack God's truth that you are just as gifted, called, and destined as the sons of Issachar. And God calls you to change your generation.

Early church historian Eusebius wrote of Christians' impact during the great plague in A.D. 309-313. During the darkest of times, the Christians' light shone the brightest and brought the goodness of God into the light. Listen to his description of the early Christians:

They did show themselves to the heathen in the clearest light. For the Christians were the only people who amid such terrible ills showed their fellow-feeling and humanity by their actions. Day by day some would busy themselves with attending to the dead and burying them (for there were numbers to whom no one paid any heed); others gathered in one spot all who were afflicted by

hunger throughout the whole city and gave bread to them all.
*When this became known, **people glorified the Christians' God,***
and, convinced by the very facts, confessed the Christians alone
were truly pious and religious.[12]

God's supernatural work in us makes us a supernatural people. Our belief is that when we come to the end of the book, you'll understand the times we live in and know what to do.

You see, this final story woven through our personal story and our generation's story is God's transcendent story. It is, of course, the over-arching and defining narrative of life. And we'll unpack this story in the chapters ahead.

THE PREVAILING THEME

At the core, the Bible tells us that we are part of the transcendent story of God's reconciling love for us. This is the ancient story, the Story of all stories, inviting us to live for something much larger than ourselves. In the midst of that over-arching story, we have a very specific identity indeed. How do we step back enough that we can see our lives as a part of this transcendent story?

A word of caution: Be careful when it comes to the door you're about to open—the process you are entering. A couple of years ago, a friend of mine committed to a process of finding the calling of God in his life. He had no idea what waited around the corner. I remember the day he prayed the prayer, his strong voice declaring to God: "Lord, whatever you desire to do with my life, I submit myself to you and to your process. Lead me Lord into your plan for my life." Marriage issues ensued as God restructured his relationship with his wife, and employee problems required more patience and wisdom from him.

About a year later, my friend and I were sitting at Starbucks, looking back on the previous year. I said to him, "You know, John, God has answered your prayer."

"What do you mean?" he asked.

I answered, "Your prayer that God would have His way in your life and show you His calling."

"Wow. Yes, I don't think I would have described all this grief and struggle that way six months ago, but I see it now. God is working on me, isn't He?" John said.

"Yes," I replied, "And the story is just getting started."

Since that day, John has been instrumental in helping a number of individuals "interpret" the curve balls they've encountered in their lives, as he continues to move toward becoming a better Bible teacher and mentor of the young men in his construction business.

PULLING IT TOGETHER

As you can see from this discussion, our goal is to help you step into a process that leads to finding your life's mission. This process is both personal and public. It will require you to look deeply into your own heart, listening carefully to God's voice in your life. And it will require you to look outward, to the world where you live, with special deference to the needs that catch your attention.

Because this all occurs through narrative—your life's story, our generation's story, and God's redeeming story—no one-size-fits-all approach exists. Instead, the approach is about relationships—with yourself, with God, with family and friends, with your church, and with the community where the Lord has placed you.

Mathew Barnett, founder of the Dream Center in Los Angeles, has ministered to thousands of his church members and other partners just north of Skid Row for more than 10 years. To see more than 100 ministries in action is a stunning experience. Matthew—whose own story is a powerful example of finding the intersection of your life story, our generation's story, and God's redeeming story—says: "When you find that sweet spot that reflects your cause (calling), it is at the intersection of your passion (what really matters to you), your gifts (what you do best), and your contribution (how you make the world better)."[13]

It's also important that you frame your personal life mission in the context of what God is doing in our generation, as you seek to be like "the sons of Issachar, who understood the times and knew what to do." This process is all about helping you to do both—interpret the parable of your own life as well as the parable of our generation.

Here's the wonder of this process: You and the people closest to you will see things about your life and about our generation that we never could. You'll interpret the challenges in our generation a little differently than we would. You'll see the needs in your community from an angle that no one else in the world can. And that's where the voice of the Holy Spirit meets you—at a time you won't know and in a way you probably wouldn't anticipate. You'll hear God's voice, and your calling and life mission will begin to take shape and expression.

Is this what you're looking for? Do you believe this is where you are in God's story right now—ready to discover God's specific life mission for you?

For the very best first step, ask the Lord to help us begin. In the words of Saint Meinrad, "Lord, let me know clearly the work which You are calling me to do in life. And grant me every grace I need to answer Your call with courage and love and lasting dedication to Your will."[14] Amen, and amen.

Continue the experience

If you have not completed the Part 1 Assessment Phase of *The 210 Project* now would be a good time to log on to **www.210project.com** and continue your experience.

3

IDENTITY
WHO YOU ARE, NOT WHAT YOU DO

"You weren't an accident. You weren't mass produced. You aren't an assembly line product. You were deliberately planned, specifically gifted, and lovingly positioned on the earth by the Master Craftsman." [15]

— Max Lucado

One evening a number of years ago, when my sons were 5 and 3 years old, my wife Kathy asked them (more rhetorically than anything else), "Do you boys know that you're going to be great men?"

Without missing a beat, Jonathan our oldest replied, "Yeah, Mom, I know. Dad already told me that."

Of course, since that day, the real challenge has been to define what greatness really means. That's an everyday adventure and learning process.

But to the point: the voice of a father—such as my voice in the lives of our children—is no doubt important. Yet more important is hearing the voice of our Father in heaven. Hearing His voice can also be one of the greatest challenges in life. The question about whether or not we hear God's voice is important because long before we become aware of our calling in God, many voices in our lives shape our view of the world, of ourselves, of others, and of God.

Wittingly or unwittingly, we allow these voices to create the grid for what we believe is true and real. As we work through how these voices shape us, we learn how to discern the voice of the One who calls us. One of the most important evidences of this process is gaining a true perspective for who we are—and importantly, who God has created us to be.

The single most important battle in your life is the battle over who you are. The voice you listen to will shape who you are.

So, hearing the right voice in your life is critically important, because the foundation of calling is built on the truth in the first few words of Ephesians 2:10: "You are God's workmanship, created in Christ Jesus." This declarative statement contains two aspects:

1. God made you, describing you in His own words as a "work of art."
2. You are created *in* Christ Jesus.

Without this firm foundation of your identity, you can't discover and live out your calling from God. We must understand that we are the result of God's work before we can work. We must understand that we live because of His gifts of life before we can give our lives to His purpose. We must understand that we are a part of God's brilliant shaping of creation before we can create. And we must see that God is the great Author of life's drama before we can take action.

In fact, acclaimed Christian scholar Os Guinness makes the important point that in order to have a calling in God's plan, a "caller" must first exist.[16] That Caller is God Himself, because He insists that we hear directly from Him about the purpose He has given us.

HEARING STRANGE VOICES

Yes, many voices impress themselves upon us over the course of our lifetime—voices with different agendas, biases, and expectations. And you can be sure that most of them want something from you.

Are they the voices of the culture and Madison Avenue? Did you know that by the age of 18, our kids take in more than 10 million discreet micro-marketing messages? Because they are more than 32 million strong and have a lot of disposable income—more than $150 billion, in fact—they are a highly sought-after consumer group.[17] Of course, our kids aren't the only target. Right now, highly sophisticated consumer marketing companies are accumulating data on spending patterns and preferences. The companies use this life-stage consumer marketing information to shape very targeted media messages at us. Essentially, these media messages try to convince you that you need a product or service, reminding you at every turn of what you don't have and what you need. In this noisy culture, it's hard to remain clear about who you are. Very hard.

Other voices come from within. Are you listening to voices from the past? Perhaps you hear the voice of your mom or dad—a message reverberating that you don't measure up or that you could do nothing right (both equally destructive). Or maybe an important voice is missing from your past, a parent who left during the tender years of development. Or perhaps you hear the voice of a coach or teacher who, in a moment of frustration, concluded that you wouldn't amount to anything. All these voices shape—or fail to shape—who we are.

In Frank's case, at age 45, life seemed to be everything it was supposed to be. As a child, he was raised in a Christian home. His grandfather pastored the church they attended. He and his wife Cindy had raised their three children. He'd had a successful career in business and faithfully served in his church. Certainly, the voices he heard up to this point in his life were all the right voices. Right? Not quite.

Responding to a voice he recognized but hadn't heard nearly enough, Frank realized that God was trying to get his attention. As he began to listen to the voice that mattered most, Frank realized that he'd missed important conversations with the Lord over the years. He had overlooked certain road signs and intersections along life's journey. But as Frank continued to listen to God's voice more carefully and closely, a growing expectation led him to believe he was entering a new season of life. This new season of intentional listening would lead him to places and people he never anticipated. His adventure in God took a new and surprising turn, taking him to places like eastern Kentucky; Santa Ana, California; and Philadelphia, Pennsylvania. We'll share more about Frank's story in the pages ahead.

What voices are you listening to now? Like I said, we all have so many voices, past and present, to work through. Yet, if we want to learn how to distinguish God's voice from these other voices, we must start by prioritizing His voice in our lives. This means having a hunger to know His voice, a curiosity about the process of hearing His voice, and a growing conviction that the most defining, transforming, and world-changing voice we can hear is God's.

ROOTED IN WHAT'S REAL

What is the truth? Because your experiences create a "grid" for what you believe to be true and real, *who you are* is an accumulation of your exposure to these inputs. Essentially, these voices describe and promote different "versions of reality." (I put this phrase in quotes because by definition there is only one reality). The voices in our lives shape how we understand and interpret the character and nature of reality. They determine our view of God, ourselves, and others, and they frame how we try to answer life's most important questions.

> The voices in our lives shape how we understand and interpret the character and nature of reality.

Of course, most of this happens in the subterranean reaches of your heart and mind. However, even though the process takes place subconsciously, it makes up your day-to-day personal worldview. Your worldview is the accumulation of information that purports to be reality, shaping your view and interpretation of life. For most of us, this is the only view we've ever had, and we are quite unaware about how it affects the consequential events in our lives. In fact, when we become aware of this reality, we see this dynamic at work all around us.

Perhaps you remember when former Federal Reserve Chairman Alan Greenspan was questioned by a U.S. Senate subcommittee about his decision-making power and oversight of the banking industry. Our government had recently bailed out the largest decimated banks, costing American taxpayers hundreds of billions of dollars. Greenspan said, "I had a flaw in my ideology; my conceptual framework for what was real and my view of how the world worked was flawed and inaccurate."[18] This quote was made by a man whom many had referenced as one of the most intelligent men of a generation.

There were many factors to the crisis that ensued, of course. However, whether or not Greenspan's analysis of his own worldview was correct or not, by examining his own worldview, he was looking in the right direction to understand his part in the causes of the crisis.

In God, however, we have everything we need to embrace His view of life and reality. The Bible tells us that He has crafted us perfectly to accomplish something no one else can because there is no one like you or me. Do you believe that? It's the truth of our DNA—the intricate and unique assembly of chromosomes that individually define us. It's true of snowflakes. A newborn baby. You get the idea. Our Father in heaven absolutely knows where you are right now, and He is calling you to walk a path into a new place where your life mission will become a reality. As you discover your spiritual DNA, you'll know God's calling on your life.

Dr. Del Tackett asks a piercing question, "Do you *really* believe that *what* you believe is *really real*?" If you've never encountered that question before, you'll need to read it again—ask it again, stop and think about it: "Do you *really* believe that *what* you believe is *really real*?"

The question initiates the process of making us aware of our personal worldview, and it helps us understand the most important dialogue we can have begins with our assumptions about what's true. This discussion of worldview doesn't come with techniques but with beliefs, and not with nifty "how-to's" but with insights and understandings.

To fully embrace the truth that you are God's workmanship requires a searching, a close examination of what you believe about yourself and the world you live in. I think of what John Adams, our nation's second president, said: "Facts are stubborn things, and whatever may be our wishes, our inclinations, or the dictates of our passions, they cannot alter the state of facts and evidence."[19] I like to think of this "evidence" as what is solid and real in our lives. What we call reality.

Your journey to discover who you really are starts with a sober appraisal of the truth about your life. Like jazz singer and folk philosopher Pearl Bailey points out with straightforward wisdom, "You never find yourself until you face the truth."[20] Jesus emphasizes the nature of this confrontation when He asks His disciples, "Who do men say that I am?" (Mark 8:27). You'll remember that He follows the question with an even more penetrating follow up, "Who do *you* say that I am?" (Mark 8:29).

The truth is what's really real—solid, substantial, and trustworthy.

A CATACLYSMIC AND EPIC BATTLE

Searching for who we are is difficult because we find ourselves in a cosmic battle. "Enemy occupied territory—that is what the world is," said C.S. Lewis. "Christianity is the story of how the rightful king has landed, you might say landed in disguise, and is calling us to take part in a great campaign of sabotage."[21] This is a clash between truth and lie. John 1:15-16 describes this as a collision between heaven and hell, the eternal and the earth, God and Satan: "For everything in the world—the lust of the flesh, the lust of the eyes, and the pride of life—comes not from the Father but from the world."

The word "world" refers to "system," the Greek word where we get "cosmos." The world we live in has a certain order, but Satan has reorganized it to lead people away from their Creator. These are difficult notions in a world that brushes aside contrasts of worldviews and doesn't permit one worldview to pronounce a conclusion like "wrong and right." However, we need to keep in mind that reality is making this judgment. We read the good news in 1 John 3:1-3:

See what great love the Father has lavished on us, that we should be called children of God! And that is what we are! The reason the world does not know us is that it did not know him. Dear friends, now we are children of God, and what we will be has not

yet been made known. But we know that when Christ appears,
we shall be like him, for we shall see him as he is. All who have
this hope in him purify themselves, just as he is pure.

This is an identity passage that contrasts our *true* identity with what the world, our flesh, and Satan have tried to shape us to be—played out through the lies that lead us away from reality. These deceptions try to steal our calling, destroy our confidence, and keep us from finding our place in God's story.

Instead, our commitment to and experience of God's truth becomes the sure foundation of what the Bible says about our identity, as well as our work, community, and relationships. Truth is *always* the bull's eye for calling and life mission. Truth is the only reality we can call on to build our calling.

Poet David Whyte illustrates the process we undergo to arrive at reality:

The Opening of Eyes
That day I saw beneath dark clouds
the passing light over the water
and I heard the voice of the world speak out,
I knew then, as I had before
life is not passing memory of what has been
nor the remaining pages in a great book
waiting to be read.

It is the opening of eyes long closed.
It is the vision of far off things
seen for the silence they hold.
It is the heart after years
of secret conversing
speaking out loud in the clear air.

It is Moses in the desert
fallen to his knees before the lit bush.
It is the man throwing away his shoes
as if to enter heaven
and finding himself astonished,
opened at last,
fallen in love with solid ground.[22]

In Christ, God gives us a solid place—a new day, where we can
see a new vision of the world through eyes that have been renewed.
Our part is to "fall to our knees," as Whyte describes, by humbling
ourselves under the fire of God's presence to experience the "aston-
ishing truth." Only then will we allow our heart, literally, to "fall in
love with solid ground"—to passionately love what the light shows
us is true, no matter how painful or inconvenient in the moment, no
matter what it might cost us in the long run.

Truth sets us on a path to agree with God's work in our lives. We
avoid becoming "like the horse or mule, which have no understanding," Psalm 32:9 illustrates. Those who choose this wrong path "must
be controlled by bit and bridle." However, when we love truth, we
come to Jesus with a whole heart—willingly and joyfully. We stand
on solid ground.

SUBSTANTIAL TRUTH

When the first half of Ephesians 2:10 asserts who you are, "You are
God's workmanship, created in Christ Jesus," please understand that
this truth is more substantial and more enduring than what you see
with your eyes, touch with your hands, and hear with your ears.
Ephesians 2:10 describes who you are now *and for eternity.* Listen
now again to God's declarative statement about who you are: *"You
are God's workmanship, created in Christ Jesus."*

This is an important starting place in our journey toward

understanding calling and life mission. If we can really embrace and internalize — believe — who God is, then our calling, purpose, and life mission — all that we put our hand to in our lives — work themselves out. Before we know *what* we do in this life, we come to know *Who* the Author and Sustainer of life is.

The result? You and your life mission become transcendent. This fancy word means simply: *"Going beyond the universe, time, and above all possible modes of the infinite"*[23] The transcendent is the realm of God, and He designed us for the transcendent. Our longings are for transcendence — for purpose beyond time and space. Ultimately, these longings can only be fulfilled in a relationship with the Eternal God. Again, C.S. Lewis speaks to the connection to the transcendent, hinted at through the longings in our heart:

> *If I find in myself a desire which no experience in this world can satisfy, the most probable explanation is that I was made for another world. If none of my earthly pleasures satisfy it, that does not prove that the universe is a fraud. Probably earthly pleasures were never meant to satisfy it, but only to arouse it, to suggest the real thing. If that is so, I must take care, on the one hand, never to despise, or be unthankful for, these earthly blessings, and on the other, never to mistake them for the something else of which they are only a kind of copy, or echo, or mirage. I must keep alive in myself the desire for my true country, which I shall not find till after death; I must never let it get snowed under or turned aside; I must make it the main object of life to press on to that other country and to help others to do the same.*[24]

Your desire for a significant life, like other Christ-followers, is wired into the fabric of your heart. And like the echo of a long-forgotten invitation, this desire calls you to find your place in God's transcendent story.

WHAT IT MEANS TO BE GOD'S WORKMANSHIP

"Workmanship." What comes to mind for you? If you're a master woodworker, you might picture a finely built chair or intricately designed bookshelf. If you're a painter, you might see a blank canvas coming to life under your brush strokes. If you're a sculptor, you'll see a block of marble or stone taking shape almost miraculously in your hands.

Whatever the medium, the outcome is the same: a brilliant work of art. Essentially, this is the closest understanding to what the Greek word "*poiema*" means—the origin of our word "poem." Just like the artisan working on a block of wood or stone, or blank canvas or paper, or the poet with pen in hand, what we can't see looking at the medium, God the Artisan can. And like the artist's subject, being His workmanship isn't static. Rather, it's a dynamic, ongoing, and unfolding process.

To fully grasp the truth of Ephesians 2:10, we need to understand the context of the verse. The verse follows a theological framework that the apostle Paul lays out in the beginning of Ephesians 1. Let me highlight the three main tenets of Paul's argument.

CHOSEN AND ADOPTED

First, *God chose you and adopted you long before you arrived on planet earth.* Ephesians 1:4 says, "He chose us before the foundation of the world" and that he "predestined us for adoption as sons through Jesus Christ." As God's workmanship, you belong to Him. He selected you. You are His. This is a very simple and direct truth of our faith. Yet at the same time, it's a profound and mysterious truth that takes a lifetime to realize.

Think of the city and even the hospital where you were born. Now think about your parents who brought you into the world. Consider the pictures of you as a baby, maybe photos of you growing up through your elementary years. Now think about the fact that your adoption as God's child is more real than your physical birth and growth, because this adoption transcends the temporal truths of who we are. Your birth is rooted in eternity. Your place is with God. You are His.

This truth is a theme throughout the Scriptures. Consider Acts 17:26, "From one man he made all the nations, that they should inhabit the whole earth; and he marked out their appointed times in history and the boundaries of their lands." You see that? God designates the time in history that we live in and the place we live.

I'm always amazed to see the destiny of a man or woman unfold before us. One such woman is Brenda Spahn, and her story illustrates the way God's designated time and place break into a person's story.

> **God designates the time in history that we live in and the place we live.**

As she drove past a prison facility on her way to work every day, Brenda felt an unexplained calling to serve female inmates of the state and federal correctional systems. She recognized that incarcerated women coming up for parole needed a place to land outside of prison where they could form a new foundation for their lives.

As she began to serve these women—at first just a few women coming to live in her home—Brenda discovered that cycles of bad decision-making had occurred for generations in the lives of these women. As a result, their children's and grandchildren's futures were also at stake. Over time, God grew Brenda's small outreach ministry to serve more than 600 women and their children at the Lovelady Center.

Understanding that God chooses and adopts us is hard to grasp and internalize. In fact, because it's a supernatural process, the apostle Paul prays for us: "I pray also that the eyes of your heart may be enlightened in order that you may know the hope to which he has called you, the riches of his glorious inheritance in the saints, and the surpassing greatness of his power toward us who believe" (Ephesians

1:18, NIV, 2004). Stop here and pray that God would help you to embrace this truth.

EVERYTHING YOU NEED

Second, *God gives you what you need to fulfill your destiny as His workmanship.* Ephesians 1 and 2 tell us that God has given us exactly what we need, from the point of our need as fallen people to our glorious calling as God's handiwork. Here is a list of what we have received:

- *A secure place of spiritual blessing.* Ephesians 1:3: "Who has blessed with every spiritual blessing in Christ in the heavenly places;" Ephesians 1:7-8: "The riches of his grace, which he lavished upon us;" and Ephesians 1:11: "Who works all things according to the counsel of His will." As we move forward one step at a time into our calling and life mission, we don't have to worry if we have what it takes to fulfill God's assignment for us in this life. We have God's favor, and we are on His side. As we learn and grow as disciples we'll experience the blessing and favor of our Father in heaven.

- *A clear conscience.* Ephesians 1:4: God chose us that we should be "holy and blameless before Him;" Ephesians 1:7: "In Him we have redemption through His blood, forgiveness of our trespasses, according to the riches of His grace." We have every confidence to not fear the future. We can rest in the truth that all of our shortcomings, rebellion, distant and betraying hearts—all of it has been removed from us. This confronts our fear of the past—where we've fallen short or been wounded. It also confronts our fear of the future—that God will forget us, or leave us, or somehow we won't measure up. God has cleared the way for us to come to Him again and again, every day, in every way, and in every circumstance.

As we wrestle with our calling and life mission, we don't have to worry that we've done something that removed God's favor. We can trust that He has our best in mind for us. We can trust His process, even when it seems like our calling and life mission remain elusive.

- *A guaranteed future.* Ephesians 1:11: "In Him we have obtained an inheritance, having been predestined according to the purpose of Him who works all things according to the counsel of His will;" Ephesians 1:13-14: we have been "sealed with the promised Holy Spirit who is the guarantee of our inheritance until we acquire possession of it." Our future is secure. We are coming home, and our calling and life mission look forward to this destination.

And here is the *coup de grâce*: Notice that the verbs are in the past tense. God has already done this for us. These truths confront us even as we read them.

Now, I need to ask you this question again: Do you *really* believe that *what* you believe is *really real.* Stop. Consider. Listen to God. Listen to your own heart. Take as long as you need to embrace these truths. In fact, pray right now again with the words of the apostle Paul, that the eyes of your heart would be enlightened to know these truths (Ephesians 1:18).

GOD'S GRAND STORY

Understanding that we are God's workmanship is important. Knowing that we are part of a wondrous and grand story is important, too. Realizing that we live our lives in the story of our culture is also important. But without a foundational understanding of God's redemptive story through human history, we obscure God's great work across thousands of years and tens of thousands of generations of families and nations. Most of us have heard the narrative before, but I want to take some time to focus our hearts on a biblical view of God, man, creation, and in particular God's intended design for our calling and mission.

Jewish tradition and most scholars accept that Moses was the author of the first five books of the Old Testament, called the Pentateuch. At the beginning of His ministry, Jesus says, "If you believed Moses, you would believe me; for he wrote about Me" (John 5:46). Think about that: the first five books of the Bible—Genesis, Exodus, Leviticus, Numbers, and Deuteronomy—are books *about* Jesus. What are we to make of that idea?

The first of these five books teaches us important truths about Jesus. First, we learn that God created everything in perfect order. The world was wisely and wondrously designed—healthy, strong, and full of life. Everything in the created order was in perfect harmony, beautiful, good, and true. Trees and bushes bore fruit bountifully and extravagantly, illustrating the heart and character of a generous Creator-God who rejoices to share His vast riches.

Into this bountiful garden God placed His crown of creation, man, and shortly after woman. This represented a dramatic culmination of God's creation: a community comprised of mankind and Himself. The future looked wonderful, bright, and glorious. What does this part of the story from Genesis teach us about Jesus? *That Jesus is the generous and wise Creator.*

Years ago, I wondered what the Garden was like when God first created it. I remember focusing on the abundance. Many years later, I now think about a different aspect of the Garden. I think of what it must have been like to know the Creator—to clearly hear God's voice and to have unhindered revelation of Who He is. So the truth is. There is another lesson about Jesus in this part of the story: *That Jesus is the One for whom we were created to have an intimate and fulfilling relationship.*

Of course, then came the proverbial "rest of the story." Into this perfect order came sin. Adam and Eve defied their Creator. As a result, everything was lost. Well, everything except one thing: We continued to bear the image of our Creator. But our relationship with God was broken, and death entered the Garden.

One of the saddest and most dramatic statements in all the Bible is captured in Genesis 3 when God asks one question: "Adam, where are you?" (Genesis 3:9). Of course, God knew where Adam was. Adam didn't know where Adam was.

God has been asking that question of humanity ever since, awakening in us a sense of how far we've fallen. But behind God's question to Adam were other questions—the same questions we're asking in this book—that have to do with purpose and significance and fulfillment. We learn another lesson through the narrative of the Fall; we learn we need a Savior—*That Jesus is the only One who could save us from the depth to which we had fallen.*

> **One of the saddest and most dramatic statements in all the Bible is captured in Genesis 3 when God asks one question: "Adam, where are you?" (Genesis 3:9). Of course, God knew where Adam was. Adam didn't know where Adam was.**

Also, the Fall brought us face to face with an adversary; Satan took up a dangerous place within the created order, now a force for everything contrary to God's design and His perfect plan. Even more dangerous than the presence of a powerfully wicked enemy, we find now this rebellion is within us—every one of us, no exceptions.

Even the "best version" of a human person walking around has an enemy within—called "our flesh" in the Bible—attempting to betray our best intentions, undo our most hopeful dreams, and testify against us at every turn.

Yet we also learn that God has a plan to confront evil. He did this once and for all on the cross as He died for our sins and made provision for forgiveness, alluded to in the description of Satan bruising the heal, but its head being crushed (Genesis 3:15). In God's narrative, then, we learn: *That Jesus is the One Who would finally defeat the Enemy.*

And this brings us to the second half of Ephesians 2:10: "You are God's workmanship created *in Christ.*" The answer to the tragic result of the Fall is what God does to make us His own. We are "in Christ," receiving forgiveness, a regenerated heart, the chance for a renewed mind.

If you've never submitted your understanding of life to this view of humanity—that each of us is fallen and in need of a rescuer—then we invite you to do that today. If you've allowed this truth to slip away from you, then we encourage you to renew your faith in His Word. In fact, this is the first step in finding and fulfilling God's identity for us as His workmanship. We encourage you to take a moment and pray a simple prayer you can find at the end of this chapter.

When we understand and experience God's miraculous story, when we know His forgiveness for all of our sins, when we've been born again to a new relationship with God, here is the truth we can claim: *Moses' story in Genesis becomes our story;* we are wonderfully set up to live out what it means that we are His workmanship.

THE HERO'S JOURNEY

Remember my wife Kathy's brief exchange with our sons Jonathan and Paul? She asked, "Do you know that you are going to be great men?" Behind that question is another more important question—one Kathy and I try to answer most days of our kids' journey to adulthood. It is this: what *exactly* is greatness? We ask it in a lot of different ways. Does my life matter? How do I find significance in the world? What is my unique contribution in this life?

We call this "the hero's journey," and it helps shape your specific calling and life mission. Don, Frank, and I have walked with hundreds of people through this process of discovering our heroic place in God's story. You'll hear many of these stories in the pages ahead.

In fact, years ago as a high school English teacher, I asked my students to consider this question: "What is true greatness?" I especially challenged my seniors to respond throughout the year to a theme I scrawled across the white board the first week of class: "What does it mean to live heroically?" As we read Dickens' *A Tale of Two Cities*, Hugo's *The Hunchback of Notre Dame*, and other stories and essays, I asked them in a dozen different ways, "What do you think it means *for you* to 'live heroically?'"

I wanted my students to see that in the hero's journey, the protagonist encounters and eventually overcomes an obstacle or series of obstacles "in pursuit of a desired object." This led us to talk about what kinds of pursuits are worth struggling for. What goals are worth risking your life. In fact, you are probably not surprised to hear that our discussions led to topics like sin, heaven, hell, and whether or not there is a God. Remember, this was a California public school classroom. Still, I tried to help my students to see their own lives as a part of the larger drama of life, reaching beyond our own generation and affecting future generations that we'll never see.

Most of all, I wanted them to know that a way exists for every one of them to live heroically. This might be different than every other person's path, but potentially just as dramatic and significant. I knew only they could find their own paths. Sure, I might help them, as other mentors would in the days ahead. But it was absolutely their quest to discover. Every day. Just as it is my quest to discover. Every day. Just as it is your quest to discover. Every day.

Recall God's question to Adam: Where are you? This question uncovers several others germane to calling and life mission:

- Are you doing what He has made you to do?
- Are you living in intimacy with your Father in heaven?
- Are you experiencing the life you were made to live?
- Do you have a vision of the heroic life, one worth risking it all?

These questions are tied to *who you are*. And they challenge us to step into the life God has destined for us.

One final important point—God often uses hard circumstances, and even pain, to get our attention and prepare us for a new assignment. That's when you are especially positioned to connect with God's transcendent story to find your calling and life mission.

You are God's workmanship. It's the foundation of your calling and life mission. Embrace it. Reconcile every area of your life to this truth. Speak it, pray it, meditate upon it. And remember the question we asked earlier: *Do you really believe that what you believe is really real?* Ask God to make it *really real.* We promise you, it's absolutely the solid foundation on which to build your calling and life mission.

A Prayer of Reconciliation to God

Father in Heaven, I see that you have made me for a deep and enduring relationship with you. I know too that my sin—where I have fallen short, done evil, and lived for my own purposes and plans—has separated me from You. Thank You for the gift of Jesus, who paid the price for my sin, allowing me to receive your forgiveness right now. I ask you to forgive me and lead me in Your ways from this day forward. Amen.

Continue the experience

If you have not completed the Part 1 Assessment Phase of *The 2:10 Project* now would be a good time to log on to **www.210project.com** and continue your experience.

4

INTERPRET YOUR LIFE
ENGAGING THE PROCESS

"Don't ask what the world needs. Ask what makes you come alive, and go do it. Because what the world needs is people who have come alive."

— Howard Thurman

Do you know your spiritual DNA? I'm taking about your unique wiring from God, your spiritual gifts, your passions, and your story—and how all of these apply to what God is calling you to do with your life. To determine what God is calling you to do, you must be clear about who you are. Most of the people that Don, Frank, and I meet have a hard time matching who they are with what God has called them to do. A lot of that has to do with expectations.

Annie Dillard said, "I see what I expect."[25] This statement might be true, but it can also be dangerous, because a lot more goes on around us than what we expect. True, but dangerous, because life in God should take us beyond the boundaries of our expectations. The apostle Paul wrote, "Eye has not seen, nor ear heard, nor have entered the hearts of men the things that God has planned for those who love Him" (1 Corinthians 2:9). A lot more is going on than what we expect.

Consider this. Right now, we are traveling around the axis of the earth at 836 miles per hour. The earth itself is whirling around the sun at 64,800 miles per hour, and if that wasn't enough, our solar system is hurling along a course set east of Hercules at 43,200 miles per hour. Even when we are standing in one place, we are moving—and fast!

Does this surprise you like it surprises me? In the same way, I think if we could see what God is really doing all around us, all the time, in creative and wondrous ways, we might have the same feeling—life is moving a lot faster than we realize.

I think we catch a hint of life's pace the older we get. We sit in the festive school auditorium watching a son or daughter graduate from high school and wonder where all that time went. We approach decade birth-date milestones—30 years old, 50 years old, 70 years old—and wonder where all that time went. Our kids have kids, and we wonder where all that time went. The older we get, the more we become aware of life's pace—it's in a hurry, going fast toward a destination, and we are along for the ride. Life's pace almost seems like we're trying to outrun the darkness that overwhelmed humanity way back in the Garden, trying to shrug off the heaviness of the cataclysmic fall that resulted in hardship, despair, and brokenness.

MORE THAN JUST A RIDE

"I see what I expect." We want to challenge that notion because the process of finding your calling and life mission means opening yourself to a greater reality, God's transcendent truth: "Nor has entered the heart of man the things that God has planned for those who love Him." God wants to lead you to a place

> **God wants to lead you to a place you've never been, to do things that you couldn't dream up — to do more than just go for a ride on this hurtling planet.**

you've never been, to do things that you couldn't dream up—to do more than just go for a ride on this hurtling planet. However, the process requires the investment of your time to explore what the Lord is up to in your life. You must undergo an awakening in your heart and mind to help you hear God's voice, perhaps in new ways. This process will help you to see yourself on God's timeline and get clear about who you are.

In the pages ahead, through a number of exercises, we want to lay a foundation for you to engage who you are. By now you've likely interacted with us on the 2:10 website. Now, we want to further explore your personality, as well as help you identify your spiritual gifts, passions, and how the story of your life intersects God's story. The practical work will be done as you complete the exercises. This will give you greater insight into the places and people God is calling you. Briefly, we'll help you examine four components:

1. *Your personality.* This includes your unique "wiring" that shapes how you process information, communicate, deal with risk, and contribute to others.

2. *Your spiritual gifts.* These are motivational and supernatural gifts that God has given you. When you determine what gifts He has provided, you understand the unique and supernatural ways you contribute to others.

3. *Your passion.* This quality directs you to the places and people where you minister most powerfully.

4. *Your story.* The twists and turns you've been through reveal the themes of joy and pain in your personal life, and the experiences that have shaped what you have to give to others.

These four aspects make up the assets of who you are—and yes, that even includes the hard parts of your story. We call them assets because an asset is "a useful and desirable thing or quality, an item of ownership having exchange value."[26] Did you catch that—an asset, is something that belongs to us—given to us by God—that has "exchange value." We can trade on it. We'll discover that our calling has Kingdom value. In fact, the term "steward" is the best way to think about the calling of God in order to make the most with what we have.

THE OPPORTUNITY OF YOUR LIFE

You might remember Jesus' teaching on the parable of the 10 minas in Luke 19. Jesus tells the story of a nobleman coming from a distant country to be appointed king. The nobleman gives each of his subjects 10 minas and returns after some time to see what the servants have gained for the investment. The first one doubled his money, producing 10 minas. The second one did well, too, by gaining five minas. But the third servant gave the original mina back to the king, saying, "I was afraid of you, because you are a hard man. You take out what you did not put in and reap what you did not sow" (Luke 19:21).

Jesus' response surprises us—maybe even concerns us. Instead of showing mercy or understanding to this servant, He judges the servant by his own words. As we look at God's design for our calling and life mission, this parable teaches us three important truths.

First, think of a mina as *an opportunity*. Few of us can relate to what a mina is. However, based on the context of this parable and others that Jesus teaches, we can think of a mina as an opportunity. God expects us to be accountable for the opportunities that come our way in life. The four assets of who you are—your personality, spiritual gifts, passion, and story—make up a big part of your opportunities.

Second, consider that *all of life is a transaction*. The king tells his servants to "do business till I come" (Luke 19:13, NKJV). This notion is more about the design of life than it is a command from the king. We all "do business" with our lives—how we spend our time, our money, our influence, our energy. This business of life isn't a matter of "if," but of "how." In other words, the king expects his servants to do something productive with the assets he gives them. He not only expects it, he requires it. Sobering. Again, this is why the term "asset" is so accurate. Your God-given personality, spiritual gifts, passions, and story are the assets He provides to invest your life in what is eternal.

Your God-given personality, spiritual gifts, passions, and story are the assets He provides to invest your life in what is eternal.

And finally, know that *your view of the King will determine your degree of risk*. Because the last servant thought the king was hard, he didn't risk the minas—the assets and opportunities—that he was given. Jesus is saying that our view of God determines how we spend or invest the assets in life that He gives us. If we see God as hard and judgmental (even if not consciously, but as we see revealed by our decisions and actions in life), then we'll always play it safe, avoiding discomfort, danger, unpredictable outcomes. Unfortunately, when we do, we miss our opportunities. If we see God as distant and uninvolved, we will squander our opportunities thinking, "what is the use?" On the other hand, if we see our Father in Heaven as generous, loving, and "for us," we'll risk our assets with abandon, faith, and an expectation for good outcomes.

The parable of the minas teaches us that God wants us to risk our assets and fulfill our role as a steward of the king. Philippians 2:12-14 says, "Therefore, my dear friends, as you have always obeyed — not only in my presence, but now much more in my absence — continue to work out your salvation with fear and trembling, for it is God who works in you to will and to act in order to fulfill his good purpose." In other words, God does the work, and that frees us to live out our calling with abandon. "For it is *God who works in you.*" That is an absolutely powerful and freeing truth.

YOU AND YOUR WORLD ARE DESIGNED FOR THIS

Young Life, an international Christ-centered youth ministry, has a tag line that perfectly expresses God's desire for us: "You were made for this." Ephesians 2:10 essentially says the same thing: "You are God's workmanship, created in Christ Jesus for good works which God prepared beforehand that we should walk in them."

Wrapped up in who you are — the unique person God has made you to be — are works designed specifically for you. These are wonderful works that make God's Kingdom real to others. God has already prepared these good works and wants you to walk in them. Matthew Barnett, founder of the Dream Center in Los Angeles, talks about "the *miracle space*: the gap between what we can accomplish on our own and what we can accomplish when we allow God to work through us." The "good works" are your "miracle space."

To hear God's voice, we need clarity — a resetting of what's true about His design for all of life as it bears on the good works that God calls us to do. God's design in your life answers the questions of:

- How will you serve? The answer comes from understanding the first asset we listed earlier, your personality.

- Why should you serve? This answer comes from the second asset, your spiritual gifts.
- Where will you serve? The answer to this question is found in the third asset, your passions.
- Who are you as you serve? This answer comes from understanding where your story intersects with God's story, the fourth asset.

When you finish this chapter, you'll complete online assessments to help you determine each of these assets in your own life. So let's look at each of these to help you understand the unique path that God has chosen for you.

ASSET 1: YOUR PERSONALITY

The first segment of the online tool will help you to put words to how God has wired you. We can already tell you a part of who you are. In 1 Corinthians 12:12-18, we read that although the body is one, it is made up of many parts. Each part provides an essential function, and while all the parts are different, none are less a part of the body than others. In fact, God created these differences, and He designed them very specifically. In God's economy of human relationships, we're not only bound by what we share in common, but also by differences that unite us for a common yet eternal purpose. In other words, our differences become our strengths when we allow them to operate as God designed.

> In God's economy of human relationships, we're not only bound by what we share in common, but also by differences that unite us for a common yet eternal purpose.

The first step in learning who you are also sets you up to know how you can invest this asset, your personality, by acknowledging that God has made you different from every other person. How you process information, communicate, and solve problems all stem from your unique wiring. Start by thanking God for the way He has "wired" you to live out your calling and assignments. Resist comparing yourself to others in ways that diminish your unique "glory" — the expression of God's creativity and handiwork through you.[27] As you work through *The 2:10 Project* on your personality, prayerfully consider how God will use you as you work with others, expressing His creativity through who you are.

ASSET 2: YOUR SPIRITUAL GIFTS

Spiritual gifts, quite simply, are the supernatural assets God gives to every believer in order to carry out his or her calling and assignments in God's Kingdom. Often, these gifts serve as a wonderful and mysterious expression of partnership between God and mankind—God gives the gifts, and we participate in their "delivery" to the very people and in the very circumstances where they are needed. A lot of confusion surrounds spiritual gifts, so we're going to take some time here to outline them for you. We want to provide a framework for the spiritual gifts assessment you'll complete online at the end of this chapter.

There are actually three groupings of spiritual gifts:

Motivational gifts. The first grouping are called motivational gifts. You can think of these gifts as a part of the specific ways God motivates you. These spiritual gifts are also embedded into who you are. While different from your personality, they are still a part of your DNA in God. You'll express motivational gifts almost like natural tendencies, similar to being left-handed or right-handed. When you express these gifts, they often describe the "why" of your service.

Situational gifts. Think of the second set of spiritual gifts as the power-oriented supernatural gifts that are expressed in various situations. God gives us certain spiritual gifts when the Holy Spirit fills us at conversion, but situational gifts are used when they're needed. Jesus provides a good example: He touched lives with supernatural power in the situations of life, addressing specific needs in particular circumstances. In the Body of Christ, God uses certain people for healing, others for special insight, still others for miracles. Each occurrence happens when a believer exercises a gift because it's needed in a specific person or group's life. These gifts remind us that the Holy Spirit is doing powerful things in and through us.

We want to point out that a diversity of viewpoints exists regarding supernatural gifts given by the Holy Spirit. Our goal isn't to address the various perspectives or to take one position in what can be a very controversial debate. Instead, we want to provide a framework so that you can work through the project at the end of this chapter and apply the results to your specific process with the Lord.

Equipping gifts. Finally, the third grouping of gifts—sometimes called the five-fold ministry gifts—are equipping gifts. The Holy Spirit gives these gifts to the Body of Christ to help each believer be mature and productive. Ephesians 4:11 says, "So Christ himself *gave* the apostles, the prophets, the evangelists, the pastors and teachers, to equip his people for works of service." These specialized leadership-oriented gifts help each Christian to become mature and to fulfill his or her specific calling in Christ. They are usually expressed through local church leadership as well as through parachurch organizations. But more important than where these gifts are used, we want to emphasize that certain gifted individuals are dedicated to helping people become mature and be equipped to be effective in doing "works of service."

UNDERSTANDING SPIRITUAL GIFTS

To prepare you for the project at the end of this chapter, we'll briefly summarize each group of spiritual gifts. This summary will also help you to understand their context in the Bible. You can also find additional resources on the 2:10 website that can help you explore the purpose and practical application of each gift in greater depth.

Motivational spiritual gifts	Description of the spiritual gift
Prophecy	
Romans 12:6	To speak forth, not necessarily predictive but interpretive, declaring and forth-telling the counsel of God [28]
Ministry or Administration	
Romans 12:7	To serve, which comes from the same Greek word we get the term "deacons"
Teaching	
Romans 12:7	To impart instruction, to explain, and to instill doctrine; also at times referring to preaching
Exhortation	
Romans 12:8	To summon in order to entreat, comfort, instruct, admonish, console, encourage, or strengthen
Giving	
Romans 12:8	To share resources and money with an openness of heart marked by generosity
Leading	
Romans 12:8	To have charge over, to protect, give aid, manage, rule
Showing Mercy	
Romans 12:8	To help an afflicted person, one enduring hardship or one seeking aid

Situational spiritual gifts	Description of the spiritual gift
Word of Wisdom	
1 Corinthians 12:8	Wisdom, broad and full of intelligence; the varied knowledge of things human and divine, acquired by acuteness and experience, the act of interpreting dreams and always giving the sagest advice" [29]
Word of Knowledge	
1 Corinthians 12:8	Knowledge, signifying intelligence and understanding of Christian religion, the deeper more perfect and enlarged knowledge sometimes given supernaturally by the Holy Spirit; moral wisdom"[30]
Faith	
1 Corinthians 12:9	Conviction of the truth, trust and holy fervor born of faith and joined with it" [31]
Gifts of Healings	
1 Corinthians 12:9	Supernatural healing of physical, mental, or emotional brokenness, disease, or other ailment

Working of Miracles

1 Corinthians 12:10 — Power for performing miracles

Prophecy

1 Corinthians 12:10 — Discourse emanating from divine inspiration and declaring the purposes of God, especially by foretelling future events"[32]

Different Kinds of Tongues

1 Corinthians 12:10 — Language or dialect used by a particular people distinct from that of other nations;" also referred to by the apostle Paul as "heavenly language" [33]

Interpretations of Tongues

1 Corinthians 12:10 — Interpreting an otherwise unintelligible utterance, typically as a gift of the Holy Spirit

Equipping spiritual gifts	Description of the spiritual gift

Apostles

Ephesians 4:11 — Apostles were given to the Church, through Jesus, who established the early church and the New Testament we have today. Some people in the Body of Christ see the expression of this gift through individuals who start works, as messengers who go out in pioneering ways—they do "apostolic" work.

Prophets

Ephesians 4:11 — Prophets were given to Israel and the Church to confirm God's Word and to establish His Word in the course of human history, specifically the Bible. Some people in the Body of Christ see the expression of this gift through leaders who "prophetically" remind people of what God has said, challenging them to apply God's Word in life-changing ways specific to circumstances.

Evangelists

Ephesians 4:11 — A "bringer of good tidings, the name given to the New Testament heralds of salvation through Christ, equipping the saints to declare the Good News, leading to the conversion of others to the Christian faith.

Pastors or Shepherds

Ephesians 4:11 — One who "watches for enemies trying to attack the sheep"—to defend the sheep from attackers, to heal the wounded and sick sheep, to find and save lost or trapped sheep. And to love them, sharing their lives and so earning their trust."[35] Equipping the church to perform works of service.

Teachers

Ephesians 4:11 — One "who teaches concerning the things of God, and the duties of man, one who is fitted to teach, or thinks himself so, by preeminence used of Jesus by himself, as one who showed men the way of salvation."[36] Also, one who equips others to teach and to apply God's Word to the circumstances of life.

USING SPIRITUAL GIFTS

Using the unique gifts the Holy Spirit involves a lifetime of learning and growing, practice and failure, and a lot of ups and downs. Consider these important "big ideas" when it comes to how believers should use their spiritual gifts.

- Spiritual gifts are *always* intended to unify. They are expressions of diversity that lead to strength and beauty.
- Spiritual gifts are *always* for the purpose of serving God and serving others. They're not for our edification, but for others. No exceptions.
- Spiritual gifts are *always* intended to glorify God, not us. The gifts show the love, mercy, and wisdom of God. Therefore, all credit goes to God. Not us.
- Your spiritual gifts are not gifts *to you;* rather, they are gifts given *through you.* Picture it this way: You are wearing brown shorts, a brown shirt, driving around in a big brown van, walking up to a door with a package under your arm, knocking on the door, then handing the package to the person who answers the door, whose name is on the outside of the package. Yes, you should be picturing a UPS driver right now. It's more accurate to think of yourself as a delivery person than to have an inflated view of yourself because of what God does through your spiritual gifts. In other words, it's all about the person you are serving, not you.

Essentially, your spiritual gifts are the assets that God provides to you, and you act as a steward of those gifts. God gives you the responsibility to manage the opportunities that He brings your way, responding in ways consistent with your spiritual gifts.

ASSET 3: YOUR PASSION

What makes your heart beat faster? You'll know what your passions are when you listen to your heartbeat. Your passion also helps you to know *where* to live out your calling. Passion is a kind of GPS for the soul because it leads you to the places where you are most alive. Your passion shows you where you come alive, and the world needs you to engage your passion for the sake of God's Kingdom.

As a result, your passion is probably one of the best clues for you to determine where and with whom you will likely invest your time. For example, I've coached my sons in baseball over the years, sharing with them my passion for the game of baseball. When my sons were just little guys, I told stories from when I coached high school baseball. I've shared about times of success and failure in my own playing days. Through these stories of my life, my sons learn to share my passion. I might be a great coach or not. I might have had a great career playing the game or not. Those facts don't grab my sons and the other boys I'm coaching. Instead, my passion for the game and for coaching means the most to them and becomes a bond between us. This bond becomes the means for me to affect their lives, hopefully for Kingdom purposes—influencing them toward God's truth. Baseball, in this example, can be the pathway to God's purposes.

Passions also come from different levels within our heart. For example, I'm passionate about watching college basketball's championship tournament in March, but I'd put that in the category of an "entertaining hobby." I'm also passionate about leadership and especially the topics of resilience and how leaders finish well in life. This is a more important passion, and one that connects to my personal story in a much deeper way than college basketball. And I'm passionate to hear God's voice and help others to hear God's voice. This passion is found in the deepest waters of my soul. Don's deep water is all about seeing people get connected to their life mission. Frank loves to watch ordinary people have extraordinary impact played out in local communities.

Passions change, evolve, and shift over time, depending on the season of life we're in, the lifestyle we live, and the experiences we've had. Passions can be very "spiritual," such as discipling to others, feeding the poor, fasting and prayer, and preaching. They can also seem not so spiritual,

> **Passions change, evolve, and shift over time, depending on the season of life we're in, the lifestyle we live, and the experiences we've had.**

such as riding Harley Davidson motorcycles, fly fishing, baking, writing, or woodworking. Passion can come out of a role we have in our lives, such as being a father or mother, husband or wife. Passion can also connect to our work, and it can even stem from an especially challenging time in our lives. For example, I know a number of men who have overcome sexual addictions, who are passionate to help other men experience the same freedom they've achieved.

I know a single mother, Joanne, whose concerns over her son having to attend a rough local public school led her to volunteer in his classroom. Eventually she took an interest in the other students and their families and made a huge impact on the community of families in her son's school. Not only did she make sure she knew where her son was, who he was hanging out with, and what kinds of families her son's friends came from, but God used her in a powerful way to be an agent of change in that community. This all occurred because she pursued a passion dear to her — to raise her son in a strong and healthy environment. Passion gives us the motivation and stamina to accomplish great things.

True passion is authentic. It comes from your heart, having no pretense. We call this a "no pose factor." In other words, you are passionate for no other reason than you are passionate! In fact, a word of caution about this: In our world of image management, don't underestimate the difficulty you might have in finding your passion. Also, remember that discovering your passion is a process, seeing where our passions evolve and shift over time. Return again and again to ask yourself: What makes my heart beat faster? What am I passionate to do? What makes me joyful? What makes me angry? These kinds of questions help you get in touch with your passions.

A word about the relationship between passions, abilities, and opportunities. Within each sphere of our lives, we are driven by passions. Our passions come from our vision of life, our dreams, hopes, and importantly, our deepest desires. We then combine our passions with our abilities, which include our experiences, talents, and other skills we've learned both for-

mally and informally. Out of this combination of our passion and abilities, opportunities come our way. Sometimes opportunities present themselves serendipitously and other times as the result of our effort and persistence. At times we stand back amazed because we know that God has intervened and presented the challenge in a supernatural way.

The important point is this: They represent chances for us to express our passions and abilities in ways consistent with what is needed in specific situations and consistent with who we are and what we care about. They function as gears, moving together and creating momentum and energy through our lives.

I'm not a physics expert, but a quick overview of how gears work explains why we see the smaller gear as the passion gear. The notion of gear reduction is important because it means that a small motor spinning very fast can provide the power needed to turn a device, which is what happens through the torque created by the smaller gear. The larger the gear reduction, the greater the torque. As a result, the output speed can be reduced while the torque is increased.

I think this is how passion works in relation to abilities and opportunities. Our passion is often concentrated, residing in the deepest part of our hearts. It doesn't look very big. But when you start with it, connect it to what you're good at, and then make the most of the opportunities that come your way, great torque results. That's when you really begin to see the synergistic results of passion, abilities, and opportunities. In other words, any time passion leads, our abilities connect to opportunities that are a great fit with who we are.

The online passion assessment will give you a marker for what you are passionate about. Again, see this as a process. God will shape your passions over time to align more and more to His perfect will.

God will shape your passions over time to align more and more to His perfect will.

Don, Frank, and I continue to work hard in our own lives to discern our passions. The process is a journey, not a destination.

Frank's story provides a good illustration for discovering what makes our heart beat faster. Frank discovered a new passion on a trip we took together early in our work at Focus on the Family. I'd been working on shaping a new community strategy following my job leading *The Truth Project* team. As a result, we had started community transformation efforts in eastern Kentucky, southern California, and four other towns. Frank's job was to lead the support team back at the home office. One day I said, "Frank, you need to see what the team is supporting. Let's go to Kentucky so you can experience what God is doing."

Frank hasn't been the same since that trip! I remember the look on his face at a meeting in Prestensberg, Kentucky. The next day as we walked the Jenny Wiley State Park grounds, Frank tried to put into words what he felt for the struggle and hardship many families faced in those towns in eastern Kentucky and his growing conviction that God was calling him to make a difference in places like this. Since that day, Frank has worked tirelessly—and with great wisdom and insight—to bring together communities for restoration and transformation. What he has accomplished as he lives out God's assignments in his life has been astounding to see.

God builds on our experience, not wasting any of it. For Frank, God took a passion from early in his work career to see start-up businesses thrive and molded it into a passion to see broken communities start to thrive. Frank has great appreciation for the way God sovereignly led him down the path of life to this place, where he feels like he is living out his true calling. Frank's hope, and Don's and mine as well, is that you too will find your own passion by better understanding how God has uniquely designed, equipped, and placed you at this point in His story.

ASSET 4: YOUR STORY

Through the online experience, you'll capture your story on a series of timelines. Several categories will help you begin to discern God's story worked out through your life:

Milestones. These include events such as graduation from high school, marriage, when you first decided to follow Jesus, personal or professional successes (or failures), and other major events in your life.

People. Your story includes events such as when you first met an important person in your life or when you experienced something with or in connection to this person.

Times of great joy. We often think of great joy coming during "big events." And certainly they can. But great joy can also come in quiet moments, and we'll help you recognize those.

Times of pain. These are times of hardship or difficulty. Again sometimes these are big events, and other times they are quiet moments.

Times you heard from God. When has God spoken into your life? Or when have you had a sense that He did? These times are also an important part of your story.

Work through this process thoughtfully and prayerfully, but also trust your sense for something being important. Go with your hunches, and look for specific memories. You might not fully understand why you're entering an event or recollection on a story timeline, but trust that it will become clear later in the process. In addition, make an effort to be as specific as you can.

Your story is where you find intersection with the story of our generation and with the story of God's redemption. The key to this part of the assessment is to understand that a timeline can speak to you about where God's calling for your life began to emerge or came under attack. A way to think about this is illustrated here:

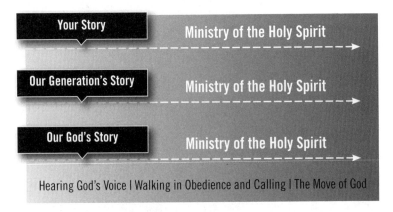

As you can see from the graph, the ministry of the Holy Spirit is key to the whole picture: God's leading and His presence with us shapes our calling, taking the events and circumstances of our past and using them to make us fruitful today and in the days ahead. John 14:16 is a powerful promise from Jesus: "And I will ask the Father, and he will give you another Counselor to be with you forever—the Spirit of truth."

You'll learn the most from the timeline exercise when you look at the times of great joy and times of great hardship. Experiences of joy and times of deep gladness become keys to us about where God has called us in our lives. Again, try not to overthink these points on your timeline. Likewise, times of hardship are just as critical for discovering your calling and life mission. Don't forget to invite the Holy Spirit to help you in this process.

LET'S GET MOVING

We've said a lot in this chapter about the pathway to find your calling. But nothing we've said is more important than this one idea: You must take a step. Just one step is all you need to start the momentum toward finding your life's calling. God promises to speak to us while we are on our way.

You are probably familiar with the most important mission statement that Jesus gave to the disciples before He ascended into heaven. At the end of Matthew, Jesus said, "All author-

Just one step is all you need to start the momentum toward finding your life's calling.

ity in heaven and on earth has been given to me. Go therefore and make disciples of all nations, baptizing them in the name of the Father and of the Son and of the Holy Spirit, teaching them to observe all that I have commanded you. And behold, I am with you always, to the end of the age" (Matthew 28:18-20).

Of course, these verses contain many truths. But let me point out one phrase to you: "Go, therefore." The words in the original language mean "in your going" or "as you go." Consider all that the disciples had experienced up to this point—a lot of it incredible, amazing, and some of it messy and complicated. Just like the disciples, whose own stories were full of complicating factors, one thing remains true: It's up to us to *go*.

In other words, I think Jesus is simply saying here that you don't have to change everything in your life. You don't have to wait until you have the time or feel more prepared. Now is the time to get moving. Start with one step.

WHAT LIES AHEAD

Before we leave this chapter, we want to give you the grid that we will work from for the rest of the book, and in particular, through the online experience that we've mentioned frequently.

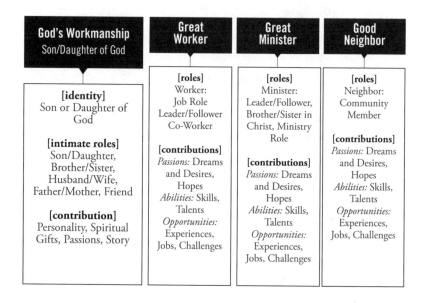

| God's Workmanship
Son/Daughter of God	Great Worker	Great Minister	Good Neighbor
[identity]
Son or Daughter of God

[intimate roles]
Son/Daughter, Brother/Sister, Husband/Wife, Father/Mother, Friend

[contribution]
Personality, Spiritual Gifts, Passions, Story | **[roles]**
Worker:
Job Role
Leader/Follower
Co-Worker

[contributions]
Passions: Dreams and Desires, Hopes
Abilities: Skills, Talents
Opportunities: Experiences, Jobs, Challenges | **[roles]**
Minister:
Leader/Follower, Brother/Sister in Christ, Ministry Role

[contributions]
Passions: Dreams and Desires, Hopes
Abilities: Skills, Talents
Opportunities: Experiences, Jobs, Challenges | **[roles]**
Neighbor:
Community Member

[contributions]
Passions: Dreams and Desires, Hopes
Abilities: Skills, Talents
Opportunities: Experiences, Jobs, Challenges |

Here's one way to picture the way God made us: The first box encapsulates our identity—which we've discussed throughout Section 1 (chapters 1 to 4 of the book). Our identity's foundation is who we are as God's workmanship. At the core is our identity as a son or daughter of God, and certain "intimate roles" we fulfill as His workmanship—son or daughter, brother or sister, husband or wife, father or mother, aunt or uncle, brother or sister in Christ, and friend. Our contribution—the works that flow out of this core identity—include our personality (unique wiring), spiritual gifts, passions, and story.

In the next section of the book, we'll look at the truth claims of good works and four arenas God has given us to display His good works. This will help us apply our calling for the greatest affect on the Kingdom—again, uniquely expressed through the passions, gifts, and experiences of our lives.

Continue the experience

If you have not completed the Part 1 Assessment Phase it would be best to complete this before you move to Section 2. To complete the Assessment Phase of *The 2:10 Project* log on to **www.210project.com** and continue your experience.

Section 2: **Good Works**

God has provided several arenas of "good works" for us, and He desires that we learn to walk in them, thus fulfilling our mission and calling.

5

GOOD WORKS
IN YOUR VOCATION

"Therefore, when I receive His nature and hear His call,
His divine voice resounds throughout His nature and mine
and the two become one in service. The Son of God reveals
Himself in me, and out of devotion to Him, service becomes
my everyday way of life."

— Oswald Chambers

Don tells the story of working with a management team led by Jim Warren and Josh Reidenger, part owners of the one of the largest accounting firms in Alabama. As Don led the group through a number of exercises—the same ones you just worked through on the 2:10 website—the perspective these men had about their own calling shifted significantly in days that followed.

One day, Jim and Josh sat with a couple of pens and napkins between them, doodling an idea that since that day has transformed their company's structure. They were thinking of several concerns about their company. For one, they were frustrated that voluntary employee contributions went to an organization that didn't fully align with their personal values and beliefs. They also had a hunger to see a greater impact among their employees in an eternal, Kingdom way. And they wanted to see the culture of their company transformed. From these needs, a brilliant idea was born both to serve the needs of the poor and to engage their employees—Christian and non-Christian. This idea led the two men to form a company-wide partnership with Compassion International.

Here's what happened next. To generate interest, they hosted a lunch to ask their employees to consider sponsoring a child in Rwanda. They hoped that perhaps a handful of kids would be sponsored. Compassion came with pictures of 24 children, all from the same community in Rwanda. Much to Jim and Josh's surprise, many of the employees at the lunch that day committed to give $38 every month for a child! Today, the employees of their company sponsor more than 80 children.

Jim and Josh's story illustrates the next step we are walking into in *The 2:10 Project*—exploring the arenas of "good works." Ephesians 2:10 says, "For we are God's workmanship created in Christ Jesus for good works which God prepared beforehand that we should walk in them."

Three words: "for good works." I find it amazing that from our identity as God's workmanship, we've been created for a purpose, captured in these three words: "for good works." God destined us to walk in His good works. Even more amazing, these are works that He prepared for us to do.

In this chapter and the next three, we will explore four major areas where God has called us to display the good works He has prepared for you to walk in:

- In your vocation.
- In your ministry.
- To your neighbor.
- To your family.

In addition, the chapters in this section of the book will help you develop strategies to fulfill the specific assignments God leads you to. As we share stories and truth claims,[37] look for what speaks to you. In fact, Don describes it this way, "It's time for you to get your radar up. Get creative about how your passions can affect the lives of others."

So to begin, let's look at vocation and the good works God prepares for us in this area of life.

VOCATION: CHALLENGES AND CONFUSION

Vocation. More confusion probably exists is this area of our lives than any other. That's astounding when you realize that most of us spend more than 70 percent of our waking hours working in a job. I have many friends who struggle to reconcile their dissatisfaction with their work with the inkling that they should experience more—more purpose, more satisfaction, and more vision. For some friends who seem to love their work, I have a hunch that they might love it for the wrong reasons.

At the same time, I know people whose work flows out of a deeper place than just the duties they perform or the contribution they make. They seem to express an aspect of who they are—through their work—in ways that hint at a larger glory about their life.

One is a barista I only recognize from a distance, observing how he brings his skill, love for people, and passion for excellence to his work.

One man is a friend whose resumé from 20 years in the United States Air Force would impress you. He served high-ranking generals and managed hundreds of servicemen and women. As he struggled to find his next assignment, he took a job at a local public high school teaching U.S. government to seniors. This year he delivered the graduation speech. He is a man who stepped into a part of his calling in a way he didn't expect.

Another is a close friend and mentor who led the effort to bring three companies public. One the best performing new IPOs of 2008 resulted in a $700-million company value on Wall Street. Importantly, he shares his love for God through a passion to see people grow and benefit from education opportunities. He makes big business deals, but he's a down-to-earth Christian with a huge heart for the disenfranchised, and he shares his story everywhere he can.

One woman I know taught for 30 years in California public schools. Then, just when others in her same stage in life were propping up their feet and easing into the golden years, she became a missionary to Siberia, fulfilling a promise she made to the Lord when she was 18 years old.

These men and women catch my attention and point out something about the nature of vocation that we can learn from: They have "figured it out" and their lives are bearing fruit. For these individuals, their vocation functions like a prism that those around them look through to see who they are. This lens reveals their passions and gifts, and it provides a deep confidence that what they are doing matters. Their work counts, not because someone has conferred a value on it, but because they inherently know that work is precious. Perhaps you are one of these people.

However, maybe you're struggling to figure out how your vocation can be where God wants you to be. In fact, you might hate your job. Or maybe you're just hanging on. But we all face the same situation, because we are in the job that we have at this moment. You have an opportunity because your work is a place where God has strategically placed you. The question becomes, as Don says, "If God has placed you strategically in your job, then you should *think strategically* about how God can use you."

In this chapter, we will bring clarity to these complex questions so that you can better hear God's voice and discern the specific assignments that fit into your life mission.

VOCATION: TRUTH CLAIMS

If God has designed all of life—including the sphere of work—then aligning our lives to His design is also an important aspect of our calling. Three truth claims provide a foundation for how we view good works in our vocation.

First, God gives us work to do. This work has value and consequence, and it makes up an important part of the world we live in. Some call work a consequence of the Fall, when Adam and Eve disobeyed God, and from their rebellion came the "curse" to toil among the thorns and thistles (Genesis 3:17-19). However, it wasn't work or Adam who were cursed; it was the ground. Though we struggle through how hard work is, we know that work is nevertheless an important part of God's design for creation.

God's Workmanship

This brings us to the second truth claim about work. In fact, this aspect of work might be the most important of all: Work itself reflects the attributes of God. God is the ultimate Worker. He designed a world that functions on the notion of work. In the beginning, before the Fall, God put Adam in the Garden "to work it and take care of it" (Genesis 2:15). Adam had a vocation, given to him by God. Today God continues to extend us the invitation to engage in His work, providing the opportunity to experience who He is when we approach our work as worship. We are made to work. Gerard Manley Hopkins' words come to mind when I think of the incredible value God places on the work we do:

> It is not only prayer that gives God glory but work: smiting on an anvil, sawing a beam, whitewashing a wall, driving horses, sweeping, scouring, everything gives God glory if being in his grace you do it as your duty. To go to Communion worthily gives God great glory, but a man with a dung fork in his hand, a woman with a slop pail, give him glory too. He is so great that all things give him glory if you mean they should.[38]

When we value work as God designed, we create a platform for the good works that He calls us to walk in. When we work with excellence and integrity, we create a way for those good works to be expressed through our lives. The apostle Paul spoke of the tremendous power of our work: "And whatever you do, whether in word or deed, do it all in the name of the Lord Jesus, giving thanks to God the Father through Him" (Colossians 3:17). Good works flow from our vocation when we work to glorify Him.

May we truly walk in the work that God gives us. And may we become great workers as we embrace His calling in this area of our lives. It's important to know that God is using you in your vocation. Even when you don't seem to experience the satisfaction you are looking for.

Your gift to God at these times is your faithfulness and gratitude.

Finally, valuing the work we do—no matter what it is—helps us resist the temptation to compare ourselves to others or rank certain types of jobs above others. To master this aspect of work requires disciplined thinking: the movie star's glittering world, the CEO's power-charged world, the full-time minister's significance-laden world. These worlds exist only in our imagination as idealized versions of work. They appear to be better than the work we might have been given to do. No, all work has intrinsic value because it is part of God's design.

Instead, the truck driver who transports consumer goods has a work that is charged with value and worth. The data processor who inputs information has work that is charged with value and worth. The tile layer, plumber, stay-at-home mother (or father), digital media manager, car salesperson, software programmer, attorney—every one of them has work that is charged with value and worth.

When we view our vocation this way, a world opens up to us. We begin to see God's design for life expressed through the sphere of labor, and we begin to delight in the gift of work. We find grace for the parts of our job that are probably more an expression of living in a fallen world—the thorns and the thistles that God said we'd have to deal with in this life. For a teacher, maybe it's a student whose bad attitude threatens to take the joy out of teaching. Or for a mechanic, it's the elusive clanking sound that prompted the owner to bring the vehicle into the shop. Or, like my friend Mitch who lays concrete foundations, it's the cold winter jobs that freeze his hands and cause his back to stiffen by noon.

We also set ourselves up for the next work assignment, often one that is more desirable and a better fit for who we are. That's often what happens for people who faithfully, joyfully, and gratefully perform their job responsibilities—they are given opportunities.

Your vocation can be an expression of *who you are*, but it's certainly not the sum of who you are. Instead, it serves as one arena where good works are expressed. This is good news if you struggle with the notion that you are not what you do. However, this idea might create some consternation if you've worked for many years to prove *who you are* through *what you do.*

VOCATION: STRATEGIES FOR YOUR GOOD WORKS

God's Workmanship

Find your strategy for good works in your job by focusing on your passion. Your passion can lead you to places and people to offer your abilities, and those abilities can present opportunities to display God's good works.

Don tells the story of one man who actually found his passion in what he was angry about: what was happening to young women on the streets of the Dominican Republic. His anger led him to identify his passion, which he translated into the strategy of working with young women and orphans on the streets of the country.

Are you angry about what's happening in government? Do you have anger about what's happening at your local school? Maybe you're just plain mad about something taking place in your local community or your local church? Examine where you're hurt or angry, because this often provides clues about how you want the world to be different—where you want to see transformation in people's lives.

94

Kevin Brown, who founded the organization Lives Worth Saving, couldn't sleep after his shifts as an officer with the Santa Ana police force. So during his off hours, he started to prayer walk the city's neighborhoods—areas where he encountered gang members while on the job. Eventually a ministry was born as others took part in prayer walks. I think about how many nights Kevin went home frustrated or genuinely brokenhearted for the problems he encountered every day in his job.

What if we told you that you can get a clear picture of what God calls you to do and to understand how your vocation and ministry relate to that calling?

But at some point, God translated Kevin's frustration into good works, borne out of his vocation. He encountered a need that was too big for him alone, and even too big to be solved by law enforcement. At that point, Kevin couldn't sit still anymore.

In fact, Frank asks the question, "What in your life makes you get out of your chair—where you can't sit still anymore?" That frustration can lead you to your place of calling.

What if we told you that you can get a clear picture of what God calls you to do and to understand how your vocation and ministry relate to that calling? Let's return to the story of Jim and Josh. In the weeks and months leading up to their company's engagement with Compassion International, Jim and Josh were leading Bible studies and sharing Christ in other ways. But they knew God wanted something more. In the months following their sponsorships of Compassion children from the town in Rwanda, they brainstormed the idea of rewarding distinguished employees by sending them to meet their children. So, a few times a year, employees return from one of these trips, which they take with either Jim or Josh. In the days following, staff members of their firm watch video of the trip and hear firsthand updates about how the children are doing. Videos, photos, and stories of their children create a time for rejoicing and celebration for the wonderful privilege they have to be a part of this Rwandan community.

Both Jim and Josh would say the entire culture and mission of their firm has changed. Do you think these employees feel differently about their jobs now? Pictures of their Rwandan children adorn the walls throughout the offices, and video plays in the waiting room to share their vision with clients. In fact, dozens of their clients have also committed to sponsoring children, and Jim has ended up serving on the national board of directors for Compassion International. Their story is a great one, a creative example of people living out their calling and inviting others into the adventure—all within the sphere of vocation.

In a similar way, Kevin Brown's life is a lot different today because he was willing to seek God about the frustration he experienced in his job. Today, Santa Ana Deputy Police Chief Tony Harrelson would tell you that Kevin Brown's prayer ministry has had a profound impact on the 82 active gangs and the community where they live.

This is the beauty of calling expressed in vocation. Look closer at these two examples, and you'll catch the secret—they're incredibly simple. Each of us has bound up within our lives the good works that God has prepared for us to walk in. Your frustration may be the beginning of your great adventure with God.

Kara, the registrar at our kids' school, makes parents feel listened to and loved, and while she and her colleagues share a coffee break, they pray for families' needs. David, with humor and winsomeness, leads the HR department of a local company, helping the executive leadership team see employees as real people with real needs. Janet, an administrative assistant for 40 years, translates her own life's challenges into compassion for those who are hurting around her, offering a listening ear and kind touch. These men and women are walking in good works within the sphere of their vocation.

Of course, joy can also serve as a pathway into finding your calling assignments from God. When you share your joy with others, they like to come along with you to wherever you are going. I know an artist who shares her love for beauty with kids after school in a hard part of eastern Kentucky. One of my son's baseball coaches, a former player at the University of Florida, has two joys—coaching baseball and influencing the lives of high school guys. My son has benefited from the clarity Steve has around his vocation and passion. One friend translates her relationship skill and strategic mind into high-caliber executive leadership that is innovative and productive.

Anger, frustration, joy. These avenues and others lead us to clarify our deeply held passions. Passions move us to action, where we bring what we have to offer—abilities, experiences, spiritual gifts, and resources. And that leads us to opportunities to express the good works of God—the ones that He has already prepared for us to walk in.

The good works God leads you to walk in will look different from Jim and Josh's or Kevin Brown's or any of the other people I've mentioned here. They will be your good works, the ones that God has prepared for you to walk in for His glory. God's plan for us is beyond what we can come up with on our own. Remember the promise the apostle Paul wrote about:

> *We do, however, speak a message of wisdom among the mature, but not the wisdom of this age or of the rulers of this age, who are coming to nothing. No, we speak of God's secret wisdom, a wisdom that has been hidden and that God destined for our glory before time began. None of the rulers of this age understood it, for if they had, they would not have crucified the Lord of glory. However, as it is written:* **'No eye has seen, no ear has heard, no mind has conceived what God has prepared for those who love him'***—but God has revealed it to us by his Spirit. The Spirit searches all things, even the deep things of God" (1 Corinthians 2:6-9).*

Spirit-inspired. Spirit-led. Spirit-empowered. These are the deep things of God—the "secret wisdom," where our lives intersect with and are caught up into the works God has prepared for us. "No eye has seen, no ear has heard, no heart has conceived" all that God has planned.

Wow!

Continue the experience

If you have not completed the Part 2 Time Line Phase of *The 2:10 Project* now would be a good time to log on to **www.210project.com** and continue your experience.

6

GOOD WORKS
IN OUR MINISTRY

"There's something God wants you to do — not sit back and watch Him do it or passively wait for Him to do, but a calling that God waits for you to embrace, pursue, fulfill. God chooses to entrust His most sacred work to people just like you and me."

— Erwin McManus

Don's good friend Michael O'Neal loves deep-sea fishing. Call it a passion. Michael had also taken a mission trip to see the struggles of orphan children around the world, and he became passionate about their plight.

How can you match up two passions—one almost a hobby—that you love and a mission God puts on your heart? When Michael did this, Reel Life Adventures was born.

Many times the networks God gives us can birth our calling or mission. Michael had fished in competitive marlin tournaments. One day, he went to visit the owner of *Marlin Magazine* in Orlando, Florida. Michael asked, "What if we took a percentage of the proceeds from several tournaments and funded a local orphanage in the country we fish in?" The idea was born that day as the two men shook hands, developing in the days and months ahead a very unique concept: "fishing with a purpose." Being fishers of men!

Every year, a great many tournaments take place in the ports of the Dominican Republic, Costa Rica, Cozumel, and other areas. Reel Life Adventures puts together fishing trips to help people experience a deep-sea fishing adventure and also to expose them to the heart of God. Proceeds from the tournaments—often with million-dollar purses—help fund local orphanages. During the tournaments, ministry trips into local communities expose participants to orphanages, workers, and local leaders—people and places they would never see sitting on their yachts in nice ports of call. Michael points out, "Outside the gates of the port in any one of these countries lies a totally different world we want these individuals to see." Michael and Reel Life Adventures offer a great example of one person ministering through his passion.

In July 2010, 13 men headed to the Dominican Republic with the ministry Don founded, Alliance Ministries, for a week of fishing and mission work. Working with Reel Life Adventures, the team split up and rebuilt homes, and they provided showers in poor communities and delivered filters that purify water for a family for up to five years. The team met needs, cared for the poor, and had life-changing experiences themselves. The ESPN program *Spanish Fly* even came along to film the event.[39]

After four days of hard work, the men headed off for marlin fishing. Trips are now being planned for fishing peacock bass in Honduras, tuna off of Cozumel, and more. This powerful picture of ministry flows out of one man's passion, creativity, and commitment. And this ministry expresses Michael's deep desire to see God's grace go to places that are in desperate need of Him.

MINISTRY: CHALLENGES AND CONFUSION

Michael's journey to connect his passion to God's mission changed his life. Today, Michael has joy, purpose, and vision. He feels humbled to be a part of God's story in his generation.

However, this kind of experience isn't typical. In our travels over the past few years, meeting people in hundreds of cities, we've become convinced that many people aren't experiencing the joy of ministering out of their unique calling. Instead, they are discouraged and disappointed in their pursuit to find their place. Proverbs 13:12 describes what the absence of ministry causes in people's hearts: "Hope deferred makes the heart sick" (ESV).

We've also learned that some of God's people have a hard time believing they have something to give. Others have a hard time mustering up the vision to give what they have. And still others give what they have to give, but they've been left empty and confused about the nature of ministry.

Finally, many people have given up the hope that a place exists for them to be used by God for a significant purpose. Perhaps you are one of these people.

We want to assure you that you can be a great minister! We hope to stir in you the belief that you have a vital role to play in God's plan. In fact, the second half of Proverbs 13:12 expresses our prayer for you: "A desire fulfilled is a tree of life." May you be well on your way to finding the desire of your heart in the ministry God calls you to—a ministry that springs up into a tree of life.

We've learned that a lot of confusion surrounds the promise that God calls each one of us to minister. One of the big confusions is around what we call the "Big C" Church, the Body of Christ, and the "little c" church, the local congregation. Because we use "church" interchangeably—big C, little c—in our discussions, we inadvertently elevate the importance of "full-time" pastor and downplay the ministering person working outside the four walls of the church.

However, ministries happen in a myriad of ways, both inside and outside the church. When we acknowledge and affirm ministries that work outside the church, we don't cause a leadership drain on the local church, a real fear of some church leaders. Rather, we raise the water level for leadership across the church, offering a model that mobilizes far more people than those currently engaged in local church ministry.

As a result, a number of us have abrogated our responsibility to walk in the good works God gives us to do. Again, we see this confusion when we talk about vocation and ministry. Because vocation and ministry can overlap at times, we sometimes consider a person who receives a paycheck for doing ministry as the more honorable worker or effective minister. I call this the "problem of the plumber," which I can explain through a quote by author John Gardner:

> *The society that scorns excellence in plumbing because plumbing is a humble activity and tolerates shoddiness in philosophy because it is an exalted activity will have neither good plumbing nor good philosophy. Neither its pipes nor its theories will hold water.*[40]

What Gardner means is that the work of both the plumber and

the philosopher are of great value. We need both the plumber and the philosopher to be good at what they do, along with their perspectives and contributions. In fact, the plumber needs the philosopher *and* the philosopher needs the plumber. This affirms what we said in the previous chapter regarding God's value for our work. And we see the importance of esteeming the ministry of both the non-paid minister and the paid minister. They might make a living in different ways, but God has given both a ministry to fulfill.

We see a false dichotomy between the secular and the sacred occur outside the church as well. Frank, Don, and I have met many people who believe their success as business leaders and entrepreneurs limits them as ministers of the gospel. Somewhere along the way, they internalized the idea that they must choose: either be a successful businessperson or be a dedicated minister. But not both. However, the Kingdom invites us to live out God's good works in both our vocation and our ministry calling.

MINISTRY: TRUTH CLAIMS

Scripture is very clear: God gives each of us a ministry. The danger or confusion comes when we think that ministry needs a name on it, a 501(c)3 tax identification number, or an official announcement in the bulletin on Sunday morning. Some ministries thrive inside the church; others thrive outside the church. Ministry, therefore, is our opportunity to serve through the unique expression of our passions, abilities, spiritual gifts, and opportunities that come from God. Ministry is a sphere where we express God-given good works, and no walls, boundaries, or limitations in this life can hinder the ministry that God hands to us.

The Bible teaches that ministry, simply defined as "service," is for the two-fold purpose of edifying the Body of Christ and extending the Body of Christ. The apostle Paul sums up all ministries with the phrase, *the ministry of reconciliation*: "All this is from God, who through Christ

God's Workmanship

reconciled us to himself and gave us the ministry of reconciliation" (2 Corinthians 5:18). Whether we serve through the gift of hospitality, heal the sick, give a word of wisdom, feed the poor, or any other expression of ministry, all Christian ministries point to the same outcome: reconciliation. The word "reconcile" comes from the Latin word meaning "to bring together again." So, our ministry brings people back to God, to one another, and even to ourselves — to become the person God created us to be. Reconciliation builds up and extends the Body of Christ.

We all have the calling to serve — at any time or place. As members of the Body of Christ, we have gifts that work together with others, expressing both the diversity and unity of God's design in and through the Church. We also all have the calling to share our faith with others, to pray and to serve the needs of others outside the Church. From these general callings emerge the specific expressions of God's unique calling on each of our lives. We serve, and we minister. I might share my faith with the people God brings my way. This is living out the good works God prepared for me. But I have friends who share their faith as an expression of ministry. The difference is sharing their faith is their spiritual gift, their passion, and their very design from God. They are also living out the good works prepared for them. But this second example is a *ministry*.

It can take many years for a ministry to emerge, but we know it

God's ministry is displayed through us to the degree that His character is forged in us.

when we see it. Our ministry is first experienced through *who we are*. God's ministry is displayed through us to the degree that His character is forged in us.

Next, ministry emerges from our lives as we consistently exercise faith in the small opportunities God brings our way. Jesus taught us, "He who is faithful with a little is faithful with much" (Luke 16:10). In fact, when we look at the fruitfulness of the apostle Paul's life, we forget that he spent 14 years in preparation before his ministry became public. Jesus' ministry launched after 30 years of preparation. If you're anxious to get moving in your ministry, first be faithful with the small opportunities that come your way.

Perhaps you know what a "governor" is? These devices were used 50 or so years ago to moderate how fast a vehicle could go. Governors were commonly used on school buses to make sure drivers didn't reach unsafe speeds. In a similar way, our character functions as a kind of governor to our ministry effectiveness. The more we are like Christ, the more effective our ministry can be. Think of it like an amplifier—the character of Christ amplifies the impact of good deeds. Therefore, integrity is vital in our pursuit of God's ministry. Good works are powerfully expressed through the life of the person of integrity.

God gives each of us a very specific ministry. Take a look at a number of the ways the New Testament describes ministry in different individual's lives:

- Paul's ministry was as the "Apostle to the Gentiles."
- Timothy was challenged by Paul to "do the work of an evangelist, fulfill your ministry" (2 Timothy 4:5).
- Jesus, in teaching on the final judgment, described those who meet the needs of the poor, strangers, and prisoners

as fulfilling the calling to minister.
- Paul references "women who labored side-by-side with [him] in the gospel (Philippians 4:3).
- Epaphroditus is referred to as Paul's "brother and fellow worker and fellow soldier, and your minister to my need" (Philippians 2:25).

Of course, Scripture contains dozens of these passages. Understand that each man or woman referenced above walked out the ministry God gave to them. The challenge to us is that we get clear about our own ministry calling and that we live it out as our contribution to the edification and extension of the Body of Christ.

Finally, ministry is a course we follow our entire lives. Like a race, we cross the finish line at the end of our life. One of my favorite passages in the New Testament is toward the end of the book of Acts. Paul knows his life is nearing an end. Roman imprisonment, and likely martyrdom, is at hand. As he says good-bye to his ministry partners, the elders at Ephesus, Paul writes:

But I do not account my life of any value nor as precious to myself, if only I may finish my course and the ministry that I received from the Lord Jesus, to testify to the gospel of the grace of God (Acts 20:24).

Paul finished his course, fulfilling all that God gave him to do through the ministry (good works) he received from God. He lived out of his ministry calling from God—all the way to the end.

MINISTRY: STRATEGIES FOR YOUR GOOD WORKS

Like our discussion of vocation, the key to discovering your ministry calling is to explore your passions. What you care about most helps determine where and to whom you are likely called to minister. Your passions lead you to serve with the abilities and gifts you have been given. Psalm 21:2-4 says:

You have given him his heart's desire, and have not withheld the request of his lips. For You meet him with the blessings of goodness; You set a crown of pure gold upon his head. He asked life from You, and You gave it to him.

Author and pastor Erwin McManus describes it this way: "The Scriptures place human desires and passions at the epicenter of human action."[41] Look into what moves you, what causes you to tear up, what makes your voice rise when you speak — in those areas, you will find your ministry, given to you by God.

This process usually happens one small assignment at a time:

God's Workmanship

- Perhaps you get talked into going on a mission trip because your 13-year-old daughter wants to go, and you prefer that she doesn't travel to another continent without you. But when you get there, your heart breaks.
- Maybe you're a dentist who says yes to contributing your skills to children in South America who have no dental services. You come back from the trip a changed person.
- Perhaps as an empty-nest couple, you hear about the need

for foster care parents and decide to attend the training at your church. Before you know it, years have gone by, and you are now the proud parents of a dozen foster children you welcomed into your house and your world.

- Maybe you are a person in your 20s, and you sense God calling you to shepherd His people, but you aren't quite sure where to start.

Let us encourage you to find the places and people that move your heart. These places and people lead us to clarify our deeply held passions. Passions move us to action, where we bring what we have to offer—abilities, experiences, spiritual gifts, resources. And that leads us to opportunities to minister. When you offer your abilities and gifts faithfully, opportunities come that increasingly fit your ministry service.

Next, consider *where* your passion takes you: Is it into the Body of Christ to strengthen, serve, encourage, and minster to believers? Or do you feel more comfortable going out into the community or world to extend the Body of Christ?

To help you get moving, we'd like to give five suggestions about how you can begin to find your unique ministry calling:

1. ***Find a good church, or reaffirm your connection to your local church.*** God designed the church as a place where you can grow and thrive in your relationship with Him and where leaders can encourage you to fulfill your ministry calling. If your ministry intersects with the church's ministry, be faithful in the assignments you receive from leaders at your church. However, they might have a hard time understanding how your ministry fits with the local church's current ministry offerings. In those cases, be patient to help your leaders really understand your heart for where you feel called to serve. Start small, be creative,

remain faithful, and stay humble.

2. *Reflect on what makes you come alive.* These are the clues to your personal passion. Because passion often tells us where or to whom we will minister, pay close attention to the places in your heart where passion resides down deep. Make the day of solitude (instructions included at the end of the book) a monthly activity in your life. This can help you discern your passions and discover the opportunities for you to serve. You'll find many resources available on *The 2:10 Project* website as well.

3. *Read about others who have lived out ministry callings that you respect and desire to emulate.* This can be a great way to educate yourself about different ministry callings. However, if you're too busy to read and research, consider the idea of "reading" in a broader sense by paying close attention to the people you meet, the stories you hear, and the places you go. Look at different examples of people living out callings that resonate with your passions and dreams. Ask a lot of questions, journal your responses, and become intentional about learning everything you can. This is important because no new ministry truly exists; instead, you'll find a myriad of unique expressions of similar ministries. Because Jesus' mission hasn't changed in more than 2,000 years, your calling will likely look a lot like what others have done or are doing. That's a good thing. Learn from others who have gone before you.

4. *Remember to take small steps.* Every step into ministry typically takes longer and requires more work than you'd imagine. Discouragement can be your greatest enemy because it can steal your energy to continue on. Start by enlisting the help of supportive people around you. Ask them to pray, to give wise and godly counsel, and to help

you be successful. Another way to take small steps comes from Bob Buford, author of *Halftime.* He teaches a great concept called "Low Cost Probes." Essentially, the idea is for you to engage in activities that don't take a huge investment of time or resources, but that give you an exposure to certain areas of ministry you have interest in exploring. A small step to help you discern where your place is—or isn't.

5. *Review and take action on the assignment(s) God brings into your life.* Understand that our calling happens one assignment at a time. Be patient, and take care of each step in front of you, embracing the learning opportunities along the way. Be willing to do any job—no assignment is too small or insignificant. In fact, it's common for people to try four or five different "assignments" before one feels right. Keep going until you find the right fit. Build on your experiences; there are no wasted ones when you are learning from God!

My first assignment as a pastor happened in college when I was asked to lead a small group Bible study for InterVarsity Christian Fellowship, a journey that I continue today. At the time I had no idea that this assignment would send me on the trajectory that led where it did. Don's ministry calling started in a small way as he took an interest in high school students who didn't know the Lord. And Frank's ministry calling was worked out in quiet ways as he listened to the personal challenges of employees in the companies he led. From those small beginnings, probably thousands of assignments have occurred along each journey—some very small, many moment-to-moment, and others that lasted years. But they came from God and shaped the kind of ministries God has given to us over the past 30 years.

What's your dream of the perfect ministry assignment? We believe you'll find the answer to this question as you take your next step and as God meets you right where you are: "In his heart a man plans his course, but the Lord determines his steps" (Proverbs 16:9, NIV). As you step out, God will lead you. You can count on it.

Continue the experience

If you have not completed the Part 2 Time Line Phase of *The 2:10 Project* now would be a good time to log on to **www.210project.com** and continue your experience.

7

GOOD WORKS
TO OUR NEIGHBORS

"Your neighbor is the man who needs you."

— Elbert Hubbard

Early in our marriage, Kathy and I wrestled with what it means to be a good neighbor. I distinctly remember praying about it on the way to work one day, when I asked aloud, "Lord, would you show me who my neighbors are right now?" What an adventure started that day as our learning has continued over many years. One particular experience stands out.

I was at a restaurant one morning grabbing a bite to eat when Fred and I met. At the time, Fred Vanderhayden was an 18-year-old homeless man. He had just aged out of the state system in California, after living in foster care since the age of 5 when his mother died in a house fire. Soon after the fire, his father surrendered his parental rights.

As our friendship grew, so did my understanding of Fred's experiences living on the street. He also took a genuine interest in what life was like for me to have a wife and young children. I learned how to help him with practical needs, including getting his laundry washed, buying him socks and shoes, and getting him help for an infection he suffered from "traveler's disease." Over the couple of months I got to know Fred, I looked forward to our times together.

As I prayed for opportunities to share the love of God with Fred, I could tell a big disconnect took place between his overwhelming daily needs and his ability to connect to the idea that God is good and loving. I was talking with Fred one day when I had the idea — not sure where it came from, but I later came to believe that it was God's leading — that Fred might qualify for some help from the state. Soon, Fred and I ended up in the local Social Security office.

After filling out some paperwork and waiting for his appointment, a truly amazing thing happened. We walked up to the window after his name was called, and with a look of astonishment on her face, the woman behind the window asked me if I were a relative or guardian of some kind.

"No, just a friend," I said.

"Well, Fred's going to need a friend to help him with the assistance that is due to him," she said. "It turns out Fred has more than $16,000 on account from the Social Security department." She went on to explain that because of his situation as a ward of the state and the learning disabilities he had, Fred had been receiving aid he'd never tapped into. Just like that. Fred's life circumstances changed dramatically.

The next conversation Fred and I had about the love of God went a little better. A couple of months later—after I helped him set up a monthly disbursement from the $16,000, find an apartment, and establish some routines for taking care of himself—Fred committed his life to Christ at a Christian concert he and I attended together. My neighbor Fred became my friend Fred and then my brother Fred. A few months later, my family and I left California to move to Colorado. I can still picture him during our good-byes, holding the kitten we'd given him from our cat's recent litter, both of us glad we met one another and developed the friendship that followed.

Being a good neighbor is another sphere that God gives us to walk in the good works He has prepared for us.

GOOD NEIGHBOR: COMPLICATIONS AND CONFUSION

First, we need to consider that compared to the two spheres of opportunity we've already considered, vocation and ministry, the calling to be a good neighbor truly tests the motives of our heart. In our job, we get a check and sometimes accolades. Ministry, too, though it might not come with a paycheck, pays different kinds of currency, including spiritual reputation and notoriety. Even if these rewards aren't part of our motivation, they're still indirect outcomes of those activities.

The second complicating notion is that many people expect the government to intercede on behalf of the outcast, disenfranchised, and brokenhearted. Of course, many reasons exist for this expectation, particularly the fact that our communities are expansive, disjointed, and transient. We just don't have the connections with each other that we used to have a few generations ago. This results in isolation—not just for the neighbor in need but also for the neighbor called to give. So, while we can make an argument for the government to provide some very basic intervention to help people—especially where children are involved—that doesn't come without consequences. We are less likely to help a neighbor than our grandparents were.

One other complicating notion might surprise you: We have the faulty notion that the church is responsible for providing for the outcast, disenfranchised, and brokenhearted. Essentially, this confusion is a version of the government problem. Like the taxes we pay to the government, we believe our tithes provide for our neighbors. The problem with this idea is that the Bible doesn't teach it. We know that the apostle Paul collected offerings from different churches in Asia Minor to help the church in Jerusalem. But those were offerings for another church, not for our neighbor. Jesus' parable of the Good Samaritan clearly teaches that individual believers are called to act on behalf of the outcast, disenfranchised, and brokenhearted.

GOOD NEIGHBOR: TRUTH CLAIMS

The calling to be a good neighbor is God's solution for the disenfranchised, the outcast, the lonely, the hungry—any person in need. We are God's solution. As good neighbors, we minister in the sphere of community, where families, churches, the sphere of labor, and government all come together. Community is where people live their lives, and often the messiness of life is expressed most poignantly in this sphere. Our role as a good neighbor is critical because we are God's strategy for meeting the needs of others.

We need to remember that being a good neighbor simply requires us to serve others—to care for their practical and everyday needs. This holds true whether being a good neighbor has anything to do with our unique calling or not or whether we ever get to share Christ with them or not—or even whether they truly appreciate it or not.

We serve for no other reason than because we love God, we love others, and serving them is a vital aspect of His design for life. God has said to go do this, and as we obey, we come to understand and experience who God is. And His nature includes serving the needy and outcast.

We can certainly be intentional in our service to our neighbors, but often we serve those around us "on assignment" from God. We don't need a specific revelation from God; rather, He has already given us the imperative to meet the needs of our neighbor.

Oswald Chambers says that our service to others is at the heart of our relationship with God:

> *Service is the overflow which pours from a life filled with love and devotion. But strictly speaking, there is no call to that. Service is what I bring to the relationship and is the reflection of my identification with the nature of God...Service becomes a natural part of my life. God brings me into the proper relationship with Himself so that I can understand His call, and then I serve Him on my own out of a motivation of absolute love. Service to God is the deliberate love-gift of a nature that has heard the call of God. Service is an expression of my nature, and God's call is an expression of His nature.[41]*

In other words, when we serve our neighbors, we prove the genuineness of our love for God because we don't get anything out of it for ourselves. We might feel good about serving, because it's more blessed to give than to receive. We might feel stronger in our relationship with God, because it's affirming to walk what God commands us to do. But at the end of the day, serving our neighbors asks a lot from us that we don't receive an immediate return from. This makes being a good neighbor a powerful opportunity because we show our motive for loving others — for their benefit, not our own.

Being a good neighbor also confronts the issue of control—particularly control in the church today. When we insist on having control, we squeeze out the Lord and His leading in the daily rhythms life, both individually and as a people. Serving your neighbor moves the control outside to a place where Jesus is in control. In the parable of the Good Samaritan, helping the man in distress wasn't on the good neighbor's schedule. But he stopped and gave his resources to alleviate the man's suffering. He did what it took—and he did it on God's timetable.

Finally, when we fulfill our responsibility as a good neighbor, we pay a price—even if we also take great joy and delight in what the action costs. Understanding the price we pay is critical because all kingdom fruit has a cost. When we show love and concern for our neighbors, it costs us time, attention, sometimes money, and certainly our heart.

But the most important reason to love your neighbor? Jesus' words: "Love the Lord your God with all your heart, soul, mind and strength. And love your neighbor as yourself." I've always been fascinated that Jesus didn't say, "love others as yourself." He said "love your neighbor as yourself." I remember thinking, *What's that all about?* Then I realized that by saying "neighbor," Jesus affirms a more intimate connection to others. He essentially says that whether you know someone or not, whether you like an individual or not, you are connected. Your lives are next to each other, now take responsibility to alleviate suffering, need, hurt, and isolation.

Now I understand how profound this connection is. We share time and space with others, we share history, and we are all part of this grand and transcendent story of God. We are all connected because we are in His Story. We are neighbors indeed.

GOOD NEIGHBOR: STRATEGIES

Good works in the sphere of community, expressed through being a good neighbor, typically come about as assignments from God. Often people very near to us physically are indeed our neighbors. This means the next-door neighbor whose son has run away. Or one of our kids' classmates whose father has lost his job. Or the "Fred Vanderhayden" we bump into one day. The challenge is staying attuned in the day-to-day events of life to the individual who is in need. When we prioritize being a good neighbor, over

Calling

Great Family Member/ Leader
Passions + Abilities
Opportuniti

Great Worker
Passions + Abilities
Opportunities

Good Neighbor
Passions + Abilities
Opportunities

Great Minister
Passions + Abilities
Opportunities

God's Workmanship

time God sensitizes our hearts to see what's going on around us. From these assignment-to-assignment experiences emerge certain themes or recurrences in our lives.

Probably more in this sphere than any other, we need to organize our lives to accommodate the infrequent and improbable need that arises in any given moment. Frank is one of the best examples of a Christian man who gets this. For many years he worked in the IT arena starting companies, developing new technologies, and making a significant impact in specific areas of industry. For his hard work, wisdom, and business acumen, he was rewarded financially. But when Frank's father, who owned a plumbing and heating company, couldn't find a buyer for the company so he could retire, Frank stepped in, bought the company so his dad could retire, and then went to work building up the business. Five years later, the company had grown 60 percent and attracted the attention of a group of investors from Denver.

In negotiations for the sale of the company, Frank stipulated that if the investors missed any of the milestones in the contract to keep the company viable and healthy, he had the legal right to step in and take back the company. What was Frank's motivation to add this structure to the contract? In Frank's words: "Because more than 100 families were depending on Wright Plumbing and Heating to be around. These families needed the company to provide good work and the opportunity to take care of their loved ones. More importantly, I'd gotten to know these families—I'd come to love them." Frank recognized his obligation to the families that his company had employed. Frank is a good neighbor—a godly man who understands the wonder of kingdom work.

Frank's story beautifully illustrates Jesus' teaching to be salt and light:

> *You are the light of the world. A city that is set on a hill cannot be hidden. Nor do they light a lamp and put it under a basket, but on a lampstand, and it gives light to all **who are** in the house. Let your light so shine before men, that they may see your good works and glorify your Father in heaven (Matthew 5:14-16).*

The first half of this verse is a design passage. You'll remember from an earlier discussion that a design passage tells how things are or were meant to be—describing the way God made something. Here, the design is that our life is a light. Because of what God did through salvation, we are now like our Father, Who is light. God's design is that your life is a light and my life is a light. This means of course that we give light to others around us. If you remember a time when you were in a dark place and you needed light, you eagerly welcomed someone with a flashlight, lantern, or other lighting device. Jesus is saying, *we ourselves* are that light.

The second half of the passage is instructive or what I call imperative. God explains to us what to do. In the second part of the passage, Jesus gives us a command. He says, "Let your light so shine before men, that they may see your good works and glorify your Father in heaven." In other words, take actions that make the light of God shining out of you accessible to others. Give them a chance to see.

Here's how I understand what Jesus says. God has been good to you—His light shines from within you. In fact, in the mystery of Christ, God lives inside you. Now your job is to go be good to others, making that same light a reality to them. Give them an up-close view of what being loved by God looks like. Help them see what being taken care of by your Heavenly Father feels like. Be a part of God's story. When you do, the Father is glorified. Wow. That's simple, and it's doable.

When you want to walk in the good works that God has prepared for you in the sphere of being a good neighbor, here are a few aspects to consider:

1. *Wisdom.* God offers us the wisdom we need to serve in ways consistent with His design and plan. His Word, the Spirit's leading and counsel, and the experience of others who have gone before us will make us wise in how we serve our neighbors.

2. *Humble offerings.* More than anything else, your humble attitude makes your offering acceptable to God—and even to others. If you remember from the parable of the Good Samaritan, the proud people passed by. Stay humble.

3. *Practical.* The sphere of community where we serve our neighbor requires practical solutions. Practical doesn't mean they are easy to come up with or deliver. But they meet needs in ways clear to everyone.

4. *Learning approach.* Most of us have a lot to learn in the sphere of community, and as we serve our neighbors in

complicated circumstances, it takes a long view of learning to be effective. You'll make some mistakes. But learn
from them and keep growing.

The invitation to love our neighbor through the good works God
prepares for us is both brilliant and challenging: brilliant because
being a good neighbor so wonderfully expresses the welcoming,
embracing heart of our Father in heaven; challenging because it
requires us to live beyond our own needs and to offer genuine, practical care for those in need. May we be faithful to obey the call and
grateful to be a part of God's wonderful redeeming plan.

Continue the experience

If you have not completed the Part 2 Time Line Phase of
The 2:10 Project now would be a good time to log on to
www.210project.com and continue your experience.

8

GOOD WORKS
TO OUR FAMILY

"There is no doubt that it is around the family and the home that all the greatest virtues, the most dominating virtues of human society, are created, strengthened, and maintained."

— Sir Winston Churchill

When Frank and I worked with communities around the country, we followed a very simple process to bring community leaders and influencers together. Essentially, we asked three questions: Where are the points of pain in the community? Where are the assets of the community? And what would be possible if we worked together rather than apart?

What we discovered in community after community was the same thing: Families are hurting. In fact, we aren't exaggerating when we say that families are the epicenter of the devastation we see in our culture today. As a result, much of the work we did was built on focusing on families as a core building block of society.

Much of the devastation we see in our generation has been fueled by a plague that has broken out in our country—drug abuse. Ask nearly any police officer about the root cause of crime in a community, and he or she will say drug abuse leading to broken families. Ask emergency room doctors what most of the cases they see stem from, and they will say drug addicts coming into emergency rooms dealing with the effects of an overdose or looking for a prescription to feed their habit. So, when we went into communities with the message that families are hurting and we want to do something about it, we were welcomed with open arms.

As we look at how we can do the good works God has called us to do in the family, we want to present two tensions in our discussion. First, we are all a part of a family—some very healthy, others struggling profoundly. And second, as we look at the good works God calls us to do, many will be done in the context of ministering to other families. In other words, we have opportunities within our own families, as well as to others.

If the Body of Christ could learn to love and serve families in our generation, we'd see a revolution occur in our country and around the world. We have an amazing opportunity before us. As we love well in our own families, we raise up warriors to go out into the culture and bring the love and healing of the gospel. As we love families around us, we make the reality of God's Kingdom clear to those who need the love and healing of God.

GOOD WORKS IN FAMILY: CHALLENGES AND CONFUSION

I shared one compelling visual picture from the Book of Job with communities when we talked about the tough times families face today. Perhaps you remember the scene. Job receives the news from servant messengers that terrible things are befalling his family. A very sad thing happens:

> *Another [messenger] also came and said, "Your sons and daughters were eating and drinking wine in their oldest brother's house, and suddenly a great wind came from across the wilderness and struck the four corners of the house, and it fell on the young people, and they are dead (Job 1:18).*

I believe that we live in a day where a wind has come out of the wilderness, struck the four corners of the house, and the ones who have paid the price are young people. They might not be physically dead, but many are dead spiritually. Young people have taken the hit for the condition of our generation.

As a result, Christians face two challenges in the area of family: (1) Becoming too much like the world that we are called to come out of, and (2) Becoming too focused on "ministry" that we miss the ministry that we can have every day to our own family. Let's look briefly at each of those challenges.

First, the family today is clearly suffering through the consequences of divorce, workaholism, materialism, confused roles within the family, and many other maladies of our generation. The enemy has been hard at work breaking down the one sphere of creation that most reflects the character and nature of God—a marriage between a man and woman and the children that come from the love and union of that relationship.

In my work as a teacher in California public schools, then as a pastor in two churches, I had to walk through some very dark days with families. In my own marriage, we've had our own challenging seasons that I'm grateful we made it through. Maybe you've gone through a divorce. We want you to know that it's never too late to begin to see good works happen in your family, no matter the circumstances. When we consider the call to walk in good works that God has prepared for us to do, we must be clear that the challenge often starts in our own family.

Second, almost as threatening to the family, is a blind commitment to ministry that some individuals have that comes at the expense of children and/or spouse. This isn't just the problem of full-time pastors and ministry workers. Sometimes our focus outside the home can cut us off from the people closest to us, through a workaholism that manifests in the church or other ministry effort. The love we express toward others outside the home must first be experienced by the people inside the home.

FAMILY: ONE CORE TRUTH CLAIM

All calling starts in our family. We might consider many truths when we look at the beauty and wonder of the family and the invitation from God to walk in good works in this sphere. Others have written with wisdom and insight, and we'll do our best to direct you to some of these resources through the 2:10 website.

However, for our discussion about calling, we want to look closely at one passage as a foundation for *all calling*. If we're clear about what lies at the heart of calling, I believe we'll love our family well, and we'll love families in our generation well. This simple act will bring healing and restoration to many.

I'm going to make a bold statement here: Every person's calling, throughout *all* history, across *all* cultures, among *all* peoples, at *all* times and in *all* places, is a variation on John 15:12-13. Here are Jesus' words:

> *This is my commandment, that you love one another as I have loved you. Greater love has no one than this, than to lay down one's life for his friends (NKJV).*

In other words, the most important actions we can take in life involve loving others. And that love for others starts in the family. If we find it hard to love our family, we'll find it hard to love others. If we start with our family—laying down our lives for family as friends—we build a foundation for fruitful ministry in every other area of our lives.

When asked what the greatest commandment is, Jesus responded:

> *'Love the Lord your God with all your heart and with all your soul and with all your mind.' This is the first and greatest commandment. And the second is like it: 'Love your neighbor as yourself' (Matthew 22:37-39).*

In this one statement, Jesus forever connected love for God to love for others. If we want to really understand what "good works" are, then we start with this foundation—love for others. Love speaks to the motivation of our heart (for others), to the direction of our serving (to others), for the distance we are willing to go in serving others (as far as it takes). This is the grid for understanding our calling.

Consider the circumstances when Jesus spoke these revolutionary words. Just hours before laying down His life for His friends, Jesus defines what love is in His Kingdom. Two amazing truths come out of Jesus' words and actions.

First, Jesus forever distinguishes Christianity from every other way of life, worldview, or religion in the history of the world. Essentially He says, for you to love, you must do what I am about to do — lay down my life. The purest, finest, greatest, most splendid, wonderful, amazing, powerful, and brilliant love happened when Jesus laid down His life for His friends — for you and me. The amazing part is that He expects us to do what we see our Master model for us.

Second, Jesus joins this idea of our love for others to our calling in Christ. "Where do you see that?" you might ask. Let's take a look.

Calling is always, at the heart and at all times, about laying down our life for our friends. We said that every version and expression of calling is bound up in John 15. Take a look at verse 14 and following:

> You are my friends if you do what I command you. No longer do I call you servants, for the servant does not know what his master is doing; but I have called you friends, for all that I have heard from my Father I have made known to you. You did not choose me, but I chose you and appointed you that you should go and bear fruit and that your fruit should abide, so that whatever you ask the Father in my name, he may give it to you. These things I command you, so that you will love one another.

With these words, Jesus describes what it means to be called by Him to His work. You aren't a servant any more but a friend. He says, I'm going to let you in on what I am doing. I want you to know what I'm up to. Then comes verse 16: "You did not choose me, but *I chose you.*"

Would you agree that this verse is as clear a verse on calling as we can find in the whole Bible? God chose us. We are His, and He has a plan for us. Add to that the promise to "bear fruit, and fruit that would remain," and we have a passage that hits the mark in helping us understand God's calling on our lives.

Then, in the second half of the verse 16, we grasp the full impact of what Jesus is saying: "I chose you and *appointed you"* (my italics). You know what the word appointed is in Greek? "Appointed" is the same word as "lay down." So, here is how this phrase can also read: "No greater love is there than this, that a man *appoints* his life for his friends." And later, "You did not choose Me, but I chose you, and *laid down your life* that you should go and bear fruit and that your fruit should remain."

Jesus has chosen us for the high calling, opportunity, and absolute wonderful privilege of giving our lives for our friends. This isn't about you or me. It *is* about giving our lives for the purposes of God and for the benefit of others. This concept lies at the very center of calling: Lay down your life for your friends! When we live that kind of Kingdom love, our families are first and most profoundly affected and changed by God.

As we talk about the good works that God has prepared for us to do—in our vocation, in our ministry, to our neighbor, and now to our families—know that good deeds flow out of these places in our lives that are rooted in John 15:13. Love well and your deeds will indeed be great.

GOOD WORKS IN FAMILY: STRATEGIES

The first important strategy to accomplish the good works God has prepared for us in the sphere of family is to be clear about this calling to love—by laying down our lives. This singular characteristic should mark us as a spouse (if we're married), as parents (if we are parents), as a sister or brother, as a son or daughter. It is primary. Love defined as radically as it is by Jesus in John 15 is the foundation for what we teach our children about character and our relationship with God. When we are clear about love, great ministry happens in the family.

The second important strategic consideration is one we've visited in the previous three chapters: passion. Your passion will be a door to

God's Workmanship

what brings you life, especially as you walk out your intimate roles in family. Pursue your passion in partnership and agreement with your family. Include them in your passion. When you are a person pursuing God and His will, you become infectious to those around you — especially to your family. As Don has said, "Do what you love, and take others along with you." This is an especially powerful truth with family.

We already told you the story of Brenda Spahn and her ministry to women just released from prison. What we didn't tell you is that that Brenda's daughter runs the Lovelady Center, and the whole family has been involved for many years in the ministry. Together, they embrace the mission of the Lovelady Center. Brenda's genuine love and infectious passion for outcast women is the only explanation for her family's involvement in the same mission.

Another example of a family ministering together involves Neil Vincent and his wife. Simply they began to invite underprivileged families to their home for dinner, just to get to know them and see where they needed a helping hand. Their daughter caught the vision, and created a jewelry business through the art she did with the kids in the community. They have raised funds to help these families and led many to the Lord. In fact, 22 families are currently going through *The 2:10 Project* to discover their place in God's story, all initiated through a simple gesture—inviting others over for dinner.

A third strategy for consideration in the area of family is character. This is an important aspect of the good works we do. When it comes to the family, character *always* trumps gifting and ministry assignments. I like the way Erwin McManus connects the importance of passion to character here:

> *The furnace of our passions is our character, and while evil character burns hot for destructive passions that consume and destroy, the character of God ignites passions for what is good and true. Our quest is to have God's character formed in us, so that His passions might burn in us.*[43]

I've known many gifted people who didn't realize that their family needed their character most of all. Not their ministry gifting, though they were highly gifted. Not their anointing, though they had that. What the people closest to them—their spouses, children, siblings, parents—needed most was true character: love, joy, peace, patience, kindness, gentleness, goodness, and self-control.

As we pursue the good works that God has prepared for us to do in our families, stay focused on your character in the following ways:

- **Kindness.** Let your words be tender and affirming.
- **Faithfulness.** Let your words and actions be dependable and consistent.
- **Gentleness.** Look your family members in the eyes, don't hurry away, and believe the best; be forgiving and patient in your relationships; listen well.
- **Peacemaker.** Be the one to bring reconciliation. Don't let the frustrations of life dictate the atmosphere in the house.

Of course, the list goes on and on. Family is where our character is forged, and it's where we help our family members forge theirs. We can't hide who we are inside the four walls of the family home. In fact, our character is revealed in the home. So, no matter the condition of your home—whether there has been brokenness, difficulty, or other hardships—start small with good deeds that speak of God's love.

Finally, good works in our families are highly practical. Frank's kids challenged him on this a few years ago: "Dad, we don't want to wait until we are in our mid-40s to have Kingdom impact. We're ready to do something significant now." It's time to get moving with your kids today (if you have children). Or, if you're younger, your actions may be the catalyst for your parents to get engaged. Living out the good works God has prepared come in as many forms as there are families. But here are a few practical ways people we know have walked in good works in their families:

- Tim took his daughter on a mission trip to the Dominican Republic (in fact, Tim says, "She kind of took me on the trip!"). Caroline's life was transformed by what she experienced.

- Our friend Mel took his son Graham to Jimmie Hale Mission to serve dinner to men who are homeless and facing big challenges in their lives. Graham asked a big question on the way home that night, "Dad, if selfishness didn't exist, would we need money?" You can bet that experience shifted Graham's worldview as well as Mel's.

- Frank's sister Rhonda and her children go to a local retirement home every weekend to visit with the residents there, to serve elderly members of the community who are too often forgotten in our culture.

We have a great opportunity before us in our generation. As you get started in your family, we encourage you to share your own 2:10 M.A.P. with your spouse and children. Expose them to a variety of ministry opportunities. Get creative and bold in your thinking. Pay attention to what makes your heart beat faster. Listen to your children and your spouse for what they have a passion to see happen.

If we can see God's good works flowing out of our own families, and if we can see God's good works influencing families in our generation, we are absolutely convinced that we'll see a revival. May God give us the grace to first love our families—laying down our lives for our friends—and then to love many families who need to experience God's supernatural love.

Continue the experience

If you have not completed the Part 2 Time Lines Phase it would be best to complete this before you move to Section 3. To complete the Time Line Phase of *The 2:10 Project* log on to **www.210project.com** and continue your experience.

Section 3: **Life Mission**

God both delights and surprises us
through the people and experiences
He uses to equip us to live out our calling,
mission and purpose.

9

FRIENDSHIP
FIND THE PEOPLE
WHO ARE LOOKING FOR YOU

*"Is any pleasure on earth as great as a circle of
Christian friends by a fire?"*

—C.S. Lewis

My family and I live in a little house on five pine-forested acres just north of Colorado Springs. Summers are glorious and especially the times every couple of weeks when three of my friends come over to sit around a campfire out back. The outline of the forest against the sky above us and the fire crackling before us is mesmerizing, relaxing, and a time of great fellowship, insight, and personal challenge.

C.S. Lewis' words are quite literal for us: "Is any pleasure on earth as great as a circle of Christian friends by a fire?" These men are my Band of Brothers, as we have called our group for many years.

One particular night was David's turn, so to speak. We don't actually have an agenda, and we don't really take turns—although it seems to work out that way. No, God was simply working in David's life that night. The four of us sat around the campfire, the flames illuminating our faces. Brad poked at the fire, Gary leaned back, rocking slightly in the plastic lawn chair. And David leaned forward, staring intently at the crackling wood, thinking deeply about the statements that each of us had just made to him.

We told David *exactly* how his life had affected each of ours. We told him how *who he is* profoundly enriches us, how the glory of his life—his unique combination of strength, personality, passion—makes each of us better men. We articulated for him what is difficult—maybe impossible—to see for ourselves, how God uniquely expresses His image, creativity, and "glory" through each one of us.

Kingdom friendships like the one I have with my Band of Brothers are powerful alliances. They are founded on a rock-solid belief in God's authority in our lives, and they are marked by a meaningful mission. Often, they lead us into trials that require a sacrifice of time and resources. Most of all, Kingdom friendships are driven by a vision of covenant love and the supernatural environment of God's reconciling work with humanity.

Let's take a dive into what we mean by Kingdom friendship and why it is critical to us fulfilling God's calling and His assignments in our lives.

KINGDOM FRIENDSHIP FIRST HAND

Experiences like the ones I have with my Band of Brothers aren't that common. Even in our churches, where crowds can be huge, people feel more disconnected than ever. Many people admit that even when our lives are full of friendships and acquaintances, a piece is still missing — the deeper experience of knowing others and being deeply known by others, of loving them and being loved unconditionally by them.

Truth be told, David had a hard time that night accepting what we said to him. I know I do when these men speak into my life. It's not easy to hear friends speak insightful and deeply affirming words over our lives. *True* words — words that call out the best of who we are. And, quite frankly, most of us have little experience hearing positive, deeply *true* things said about who God has made us to be.

> Quite frankly, most of us have little experience hearing positive, deeply *true* things said about who God has made us to be.

For me, these past years of friendship with Gary, David, and Brad have made me a better friend and colleague in other areas of my life and ministry. I'm also deeply grateful for my friendship and co-laboring relationships with Don and Frank, with whom I am writing this book. The three of us are on assignment together — we also spend time *around the fire*; in just a few years, we've become close friends. We trust each other, know each other's strengths and struggles, and experience friendship with God in our midst.

At times, most of us face insurmountable challenges — interwoven with our destiny — and we realize how much we need the people closest to us. We need friends who will travel with us, battle alongside us, and share the journey with us. This is what a covenant community is all about.

In Chapter 3, we discussed how our identity as God's workmanship provides the foundation of our calling and life mission. Similarly, deep friendships — formed around our calling and life mission — are essential for us to understand who we are in Christ, what gifts and passions we possess, and the places where and people to whom God calls us.

Friendship is both a means and an end in God's plan for each of our lives. In this chapter, we want to lay out a pathway for finding deep friendships or for taking the friendships you already have and transforming them around life mission and purpose. First, let's explore one of the most important concepts in the Bible, covenant, to understand the foundation of Kingdom friendship.

COVENANT RELATIONSHIPS

The word "covenant" is our best attempt at an English translation of a Hebrew word that refers to God's initiative in relating to His people. That word is *chesed*, and we also translate it as "lovingkindness." However, these words don't even come close to expressing what true *chesed* means. At the root, the word speaks of faithfulness, describing how we're connected to one another at the deepest places. At the core of the biblical understanding of relationships, covenant describes the centrality of promises and vows that protect our relationships with each other and with God. This understanding is vital to a Christian worldview and a primary theme throughout Scripture.

We understand *chesed* through our reading of the Israelites' experience of God's faithfulness, illustrating the special relationship of unmerited favor they received from their covenant-keeping God. God's actions were always in the Jewish people's best interest. *Chesed* was literally the "doing of the promise" between the two parties who had entered into the covenant.

Do you remember the formal "signing" of the contract between God and the Israelites? The signing of the covenant was referred to as "the cutting of the covenant." The tradition, common among both the Israelites and neighboring people groups, required that the two parties entering into the covenant pass between the two halves of a sacrificed animal. The imagery represented the commitment of each party to fulfill his responsibilities to always act for the good of the other party. By walking between the sacrificed animal halves, each was saying, "May it thus be done to me if I do not fulfill the conditions of this covenant."[38]

But something different happened with Abraham and the Lord. Maybe you remember the scene in Genesis 15. Instead of both Abraham and the Lord passing between the two halves of the sacrifice, God caused Abraham to fall into a deep sleep, and only the Lord passed between the halves. In effect, God was saying, "The provision for you to fulfill your promises to Me is found in Me alone." This mysterious scene between Abraham and the Lord becomes clear at the cross, where God Himself provided Jesus—the sacrifice required to secure the covenant relationship for salvation. And now the Holy Spirit daily empowers us to live out our promises and vows before God and man.

What do we learn from all this? That God Himself provides for us all that is required of us. This is the heart of relationship with God—to receive the provision *from Him* so we can give our faithfulness *to Him*.

When God fulfills His promises, it speaks of His immutability, omnipotence, and lovingkindness. To us, Kingdom friendship is a completely new experience—even a new reality. God's faithfulness to us opens the door to us to know a supernatural kind of friendship. What we learn from God's design for Kingdom friendship is that our commitments to one another, empowered by God's enabling presence, create an atmosphere for deep relationships.

In fact, if you look at the entire Bible through this grid of covenant relationships, a lot will come into focus for you. For example, when you look closely at the 10 Commandments that God gave to the Israelites, you'll see this grid of relationships. Each of the commandments protects relationships—with God and with one another. God jealously guards His relationships with each of us, with His people, as well as our relationships with one another. At the center of eternity is the Triune God, in perfect relationship, marked by love and submission. At the center of creation is the Triune God, inviting us into a relationship that promises to fulfill our deepest longings and purposes.

Commitment is the living out of covenant. Have you noticed how fulfilled promises surprise the world? When I attended my nephew's wedding a few summers ago, the guests experienced a lot of joy seeing the bride and groom make their vows to one another. At the same time, people expressed a kind of awe to see those same vows still being fulfilled after 50 years in the grandparents' presence at the wedding. In fact, when introduced at the reception, spontaneous applause erupted from the guests, providing a beautiful affirmation of the power of commitment—the living out of the marriage covenant.

We know the joy in the *making* of a vow. But, we are in *awe* at the fulfilling of a vow. God's very nature is reflected in fulfilled promises and vows. May we be a people who know both the joy and the awe of fulfilled promises.

We know the joy in the *making* of a vow. But, we are in *awe* at the fulfilling of a vow.

COVENANT AND THE COMMUNITY

We often struggle to understand the community aspect of the gospel. In the expression of Christian faith in our culture, we usually say that the gospel is communicated primarily as a relationship between God and the individual believer. This personal nature of our relationship with Him is certainly an important aspect of God's redemptive work. However, perhaps the world's difficulty recognizing Christ is related to lack of experience of the biblical sense of community, which is grounded in this idea of covenant.

As Don, Frank, and I have had conversations with folks around the country, we're convinced that people aren't finding that experience of community in churches today. People feel isolated. They know a lot of people but readily admit they don't experience depth in their relationships. Yet every aspect of what Jesus said to the crowds, to His disciples, and to the enemies of God's truth was rooted in the idea that God had chosen a group of people to be His own. Corporateness, togetherness, and community are ideas that lie at the heart of the biblical view of relationships.

The covenant community of Kingdom friendship provides a place where we experience the grace of God and where we challenge one another to be committed to live from the deep places of our heart. Successful friendships involve groups of committed individuals who learn to travel together in the direction of God's leadership. Over time, this results in the development of a legacy that affects not only the assignments we find ourselves in (work, family, neighborhood), but every relationship in our lives. My Kingdom friendships with Frank and Don make me a better husband, a better father, a better leader, and a better person.

This legacy also influences the culture in the years ahead. It provides an inheritance for our children that moth and thief can't destroy (see Luke 12:33-34). And in a mysterious and wondrous way, this legacy of Kingdom friendship shows forth the story of God through our lives into eternity. Hebrews 11, the "hall of fame" of God's courageous people of faith, says to us, "What we do matters, and will be remembered throughout eternity." We aim at God's bull's eye when we make relationships the very center of our purpose on earth.

We *must* travel with friends. The key is community that produces deep and long-lasting relationships. These Kingdom relationships are covenant communities marked by these foundational truths:

- Covenant friendship unites us by a shared mission so that we live significant lives, leaving a legacy for our families, friends, communities, and generations to come.
- Covenant friendship provides a safe place for us to experience God's redemption, where we also learn how to give and receive God's Kingdom love.

COVENANT FRIENDSHIP: MISSION AND LEGACY

Mission is the first essential ingredient in establishing Kingdom friendship. The technical definition for mission describes the purpose of a group of people "sent to a foreign country to conduct negotiations, perform special tasks, or to provide services."[44] A mission is also a "combat operation or task assigned to an individual or group."[45] I love those definitions because they speak of purpose and of specific assignments tied into a larger story. Kingdom friendship happens in the context of what God is doing in the larger story of our generation and in His overall story.

We can find the secret to establishing this kind of friendship in the words of Jesus when he tells us, that in order to become His brother, we must surrender and do the will of the Father (see Mark 3:35). This is stunning! You'll remember, a crowd is around him inside a home or a business, and from outside his mother and brothers send word to Jesus that they've arrived. At this point, Jesus turns to all those seated around him and says, "Who are my mother and brothers? Here they are! Whoever does the will of my Father in heaven is my brother and sister and mother." Mission means doing the will of Jesus—and founding our Kingdom friendships on a jealous commitment to Jesus' will for our lives.

I find it interesting that Jesus also, in an indirect way, defines God's will for us. Look again at the scene. Jesus' friends were all doing the same thing: they were *with Him*. We've done a lot to confuse each other about God's will for our lives. I'll be the first to say that following Jesus requires that we get moving, but if we're not just *with Jesus* first, then we're missing what it means to build Kingdom relationships.

I hope you got that.

Following Jesus creates bonds and relationships that are supernatural, with Jesus in the center. We can say with certainty that our mission is to do the will of our Father in heaven and to establish a context for our friendships that places God's will in the center.

Perhaps we've left this critical and essential truth out of our efforts to establish deep friendships: Doing Jesus' will produces friends that are better than brothers? If this statement is true, then how do we live out a mission with whom we are traveling?

Because we're attempting to live out a *mission*, we recognize that the context of our relationships is warfare, a "combat operation or task assigned to an individual or group." (We'll discuss this in more depth in the next chapter). For now, understand that the definition for mission indicates we are living behind enemy lines, and we are working to accomplish the mission's objectives. Remember, "conduct negotiations, perform special tasks, or provide services." Think creatively what these three descriptions might mean for your covenant friendships' activities.

For example, for me, "conduct negotiations" describes how my friends help me find agreement with divisive people, as well as how I can "negotiate" my life through difficult places, and even how I might embrace certain truths that seem to be just out of my reach. My deepest friends reason with me and help me think through all that is most true about my life, about God, and about others. Similarly, "special tasks" are those that we're each uniquely gifted to provide. And "services" can be the practical ways we serve each other.

You get the idea. My guess is that these key phrases can give you a completely new framework for viewing your time with your friends and for understanding the context of your interactions. Mutual commitment to this kind of group provides a purpose rooted in eternity—friendship that God greatly blesses.

Friendships on mission are also highly strategic. Just like Special Forces soldiers on a mission together, each individual has a role to play; together the group can accomplish a mission that would be impossible to accomplish alone. In fact, Don describes his friendship with Tim, a friend he has walked with for 25 years. Over that time, they've been blessed with a solid friendship. But in the last three years, their friendship has developed an "on mission" context. As a result, their friendship has deepened.

This makes the environment of friendships a safe place and encourages us to "give voice" to what affects us down deep. This kind of atmosphere should keep us from judging one another or trying to prescribe what godliness should look like in a certain situation. We know that we don't already have the right answers, and instead we learn to listen closely to each other and to the Lord.

This also makes the environment of friendships a strategic place. Most importantly, the process of deepening our Kingdom friendships helps us to discern God's voice, apply His Word to our lives, and move forward into actions that are significant and meaningful. Kingdom friends share a common mission at an uncommon time in history. This mission is the living out of the transcendent story through the daily events of our lives at home, work, and in our communities. Mission is dangerous yet purposeful—and deeply liberating and life-giving—when we step into God's will for each of our lives.

All of this means that in covenant friendships we move together down the same road, even if we are in different places individually or assigned to different areas of the battle. The results are "mission-driven" friendships where God produces the fruit of labor. He also takes our mistakes, failures, and weaknesses to become instruments of His purposes on the earth.

The risk in what I'm describing here is that we "over-spiritualize" our friendships. I've been in friendships where it seemed we always had to be talking about God or studying the Bible or doing something related to church or ministry. That's not what we're talking about. Kingdom friendships are natural, touch on every area of interest and passion we have, and express the whole experience of what it means to be alive. These covenant friendships are both significant and fun. In fact, I took a trip recently with Don and Frank that illustrates what I mean.

A few months ago, the three of us went pig hunting. If you live in the South, you didn't bat an eye at that last statement. But for this guy who grew up in California and who now lives in Colorado, hearing the word "hunting" and "pig" in the same sentence didn't make sense. The infrequent times that I do go hunting, I might hunt elk. But pig? Yet that's what we did—and what a blast we had together.

I once heard someone say, "Treat your family as friends and your friends as family." One person I know who has done that brilliantly is Don. Don's family is a beautiful picture of kingdom friendship on mission. One way that Don lives this out is by supporting his wife Susie's calling, illustrated in the poignant story below. Out of each of their relationships with God, their covenant marriage relationship, and their friendship with each other flow friendships with the young people Susie ministers to. Here is Don telling the story in his own words:

> *"I believe God uses all types of strategies to bring people into a relationship with Him, but for us it is relational ministry that works. My wife Susie is a 51-year-old with a huge heart for teenage girls.*

In Susie's early 20s she served on the staff of Young Life, a relational ministry to teenagers. She stepped away from direct ministry to kids when we started a family. At age 48, Susie was asked to lead a cabin of middle school girls for a week at a Young Life camp in Florida. She hesitantly agreed but had many concerns. The biggest one being, "are these girls going to want someone my age in their cabin?" I reminded her that kids just want to be known and loved. As the week unfolded she was reminded over and over of that simple truth. Deep bonds formed between Susie and her girls as they processed the Gospel and talked about what was really going on in their lives. The relationships that began that week in 2008 continue to this day. These precious, yet complicated and sometimes insecure, middle school girls have become young women searching for God. They have responded to God's love for them expressed through Susie and will never be the same.

Our house is a center for gatherings of young girls, cool college-age Young Life leaders, as well as parents looking for advice from her. When she runs errands, she asks a couple of girls to go along. Most Sundays we have at least one of her girls, most of whom have no church affiliation, go to church wih us. In fact, the other day we had the joy of serving communion for the first time to a girl who Susie had befriended and led to Christ.

To top it off, Susie, a division one runner at UC Berkeley in the early 80's, is an assistant track and cross country coach at the school where she leads Young Life. Through her passions and giftings, she is impacting countless kids a week, listening to them, learning about their lives, and sharing the hope found only in Christ. God has Susie in her Zone, the perfect mission for her because of how He gifted her. She has been ambushed by God and is joyfully obeying His calling."

Did you catch the flow in this story? Through Susie's relationships with God, young people in their community are caught up in friendship with her—and eventually, friendship with God and His greater story of redemption. All this occurs around a simple idea: *Take people with you.* Taking people with you applies in practical ways what Henri Nouwen called the ministry of presence:

> *More and more, the desire grows in me simply to walk around, greet people, enter their homes, sit on their doorsteps, play ball, throw water, and be known as someone who wants to live with them. It is a privilege to have the time to practice this simple ministry of presence. But I wonder more and more if the first thing shouldn't be to know people by name, to eat and drink with them, to listen to their stories and tell your own, and to let them know with words, handshakes, and hugs that you do not simply like them, but truly love them.*[46]

Susie fulfills her calling—reaching out to and loving junior high students—because of the support of *community*, in this case with Don's support as a husband and friend. Whether lived out with our family or others, friendship provides the environment for fruitful, meaningful, and rewarding ministry. Friendship is the environment of mission.

WHAT HINDERS YOU

We've talked about God-centered relationships that produce mission-driven friendship. If you're like Don, Frank, and me, you've probably wrestled with the challenge to experience these kinds of Kingdom friendships. But only Christ's redemptive work changes us into the likeness of Christ, empowering us to be the kind of people who live out Kingdom friendships.

These redemptive friendships won't happen before we begin creating safe communities where people can address their fears, hopes, and dreams. When one of us has an argument with a spouse, we should be able talk about it in the raw language that describes the pain we feel at the time. This is important, because when we feel safe, we can go to the places in our heart where we can express our fear, pride, love, hate, and hope honestly and without fear of judgment. This safe place provides an environment for Kingdom redemption.

In fact, experiencing God's redemption is an essential element to walking into our calling and destiny. The greatest challenge facing people today is what I call the scarcity of "habitat." Almost like an endangered species whose numbers have declined from the shrinking of habitat, so are the numbers of people who have truly experienced the healing redemption of the gospel. The habitat for redemptive relationships is rare in many places. Redemptive friendships challenge us to a new understanding of covenant love. This kind of environment provides the place to "confess our sins," and where we can receive forgiveness and restoration.

> **In fact, experiencing God's redemption is an essential element to walking into our calling and destiny.**

Before we end our discussion on covenant friendships, let's address one huge barrier to forming these redemptive relationships. I call it the fashion of our fig leaf. I believe the primary barrier to experiencing the shared life is shame. And shame produces in us an independent spirit, rather than one of interdependence. This is summed up in Satan's lie to us: "You can do this on your own."

You remember the Bible's description of Adam and Eve's sin on that fateful day (see Genesis 3). They hid from God when they "heard the sound of the Lord God walking in the garden during the cool of the day."

God came looking for them to enjoy His relationship with them.

Instead, in fear and shame Adam and Eve hid from God. God called out to Adam, "Where are you?"

Adam's response might be the saddest words in all the Bible: "I *heard your voice* in the garden, and I was *afraid* because I was *naked*; and I *hid* myself" (my italics). We've been hiding ever since! Shame rarely rears its ugly head. Instead, it plays itself out in pride, independence, and isolation. But God has a better plan.

Instead of shame and isolation, God places us in relationships with others. By His design, our differences are intended to provide intimacy, security, and strength. However, we must consistently live with God's design to benefit from it. In other words, our differences can either be a blessing or a curse, depending on how we manage them in our relationships.

> Instead of shame and isolation, God places us in relationships with others. By His design, our differences are intended to provide intimacy, security, and strength.

Our good friend and colleague, Rodney Cox of Ministry Insights, describes this as the Law of Differences. This concept provides a great framework for applying these truth claims to the issue of calling. Here is the "Big Idea:" *It is only when we learn to value and appreciate differences as God's design will we experience the fullness of what He has intended for us.* This big idea is undergirded by four principles:

1. God's design is intended for different parts to be arranged to produce a whole.
2. We don't need to strive to become something other than what we are in order to belong.
3. We don't need people around us who act and think like we do.
4. God "sets" or "arranges" the members of His body as He wants them to be.

However, the way we manage differences can lead to life or death. Using these four principles, Rodney unpacks this important notion—that differences are at the heart of either despair or hope. Here's the idea expressed in a more graphic way:

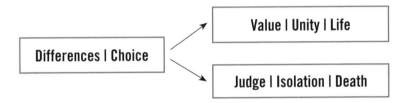

To put this in practical terms, as you build Kingdom friendships in the days ahead, affirm the differences you have with the people God has brought into your life. Value differences, and strive for unity. That will bring hope and life to your calling and mission.

Friendship is the environment where mission is most powerfully expressed. May God continue to lead you to deeper friendships with your family and friends He brings into your life.

Continue the experience

It is almost time to print your S.O.L.O. Workbook that is designed to be used during your day of solitude time. If you have not completed Phase 1 and 2 of the online interactions now would be a good time to complete them. Log on to **www.210project.com** to continue your experience.

10

OPPOSITION
WARFARE AND THE CHALLENGE OF WEAKNESS

God employs several translators; some pieces are translated by age, some by sickness, some by war, some by justice.

— John Donne

As we've been writing this book, Frank and his wife Cindy experienced one of the most difficult events parents can face. Jessica, their beautiful 14-year-old daughter, was diagnosed with a rare form of cancer. After a brutal, six-month struggle against this enemy, Frank and his family have this long battle behind them. Today, Jessica, a vibrant young woman in high school with a heart full of wonder and insight, is officially in remission, with a promising future ahead of her.

Trials can so easily threaten our pursuit and fulfillment of our calling. Trials often fall into one of two categories: warfare and weakness. At the core of both battles—one an external conflict against the Enemy of our souls and the other an internal struggle to deal with the vulnerability of our soul—is the choice between truth and lie. The trajectory of our life with God rises and falls on our ability to choose God's truth over the many lies that pervade our world.

During our times of struggle, we might experience a kind of fog of the soul. I'm sure Frank and Cindy did as they almost helplessly—at least from a human perspective—watched Jessica go through diagnosis and treatment. Trials big and small make our lives heavy, our shoulders hunch over, and we see only the next step in front of us. Even reassuring words of friends and family members can seem like hollow encouragement. In these times, a choice lies before us: believe the truth, or accept the lie.

Perhaps my words sound harsh. I've sat with people for many hours listening, empathizing, encouraging, and counseling the best I knew how. I can tell you my experience has taught me this: God's Word embraced as a whole view of life offers the only way through the inevitable warfare and unavoidable weakness that we face in our lives.

So, it won't surprise you then that the Enemy targets us. Satan will do anything he can to block, dissuade, discourage, hinder, obstruct, confound, confuse, impede, deter, thwart, prevent, fluster—really to *bedevil* us from our calling. We are targets, and the sooner we live consistent with that reality, the sooner we live out the assignments God calls us to engage.

Because we inhabit these frail bodies, it shouldn't surprise us that the inclinations of our natural mind lead us to believe silly myths about what is true and what is not true. We engage in gossip, fear future events, look at others as stepping stones in pursuit of our own goals and aspirations, think too much of ourselves and too little of others (and hardly ever of God), and struggle with the physical impulses and appetites of our bodies. Simply put, we're just not very good at managing our own lives. We inevitably have one or more weaknesses connected to our natural mind that require us to learn to trust God and allow His strength to overcome our otherwise natural—and often quite dangerous—minds.

To interpret the parable of our lives, we must have a clear understanding of the inevitability of warfare and the challenge of weakness. John Donne, the great Christian poet of the 16th century, said, "God employs several translators; some pieces are translated by age, some by sickness, some by war, some by justice."[46] If we are careful to observe and reflect, we'll find that God uses these two challenges—warfare and weakness—as "translators" to decipher God's very best for our lives.

THE INEVITABILITY OF WARFARE

In the process of discovering our calling, we must first be sober that this side of heaven is fraught with danger and violence. The well-known writer and apologist G.K. Chesterton explained the paradoxical challenge we face every day in living in this world that is both our home and the battlefield of our lives: "We have to feel the universe at once as an ogre's castle, to be stormed, and yet as our own cottage, to which we can return at evening."[48]

Isn't that the irony? We go home to our families, and the battle rages between ourselves and our teenager or spouse, no matter how certain we are that the Enemy is not within. And we find that the battle rages even within our minds as we struggle with our bad habits, irritations, or mood swings. And just when we think that the enemy couldn't be any closer, the battle rages within our own heart, as we struggle with deep questions about ourselves, life, or God.

For many reasons, understanding the warfare we battle has changed the way I counsel and coach people looking for their next assignment in God's story. I've stopped trying to help them escape from these battles. The apostle Paul said, "For our struggle is not against flesh and blood, but against the rulers, against the powers, against the world forces of this darkness, against the spiritual forces of wickedness in the heavenly places" (Ephesians 6:12). In other words, we are not our own worst enemy—our own flesh and blood is not the core issue. The Enemy is.

Just as certainly, our rebellious teenage son or daughter is not, our neurotic neighbor is not, and our egocentric boss is not the enemy. Instead, the struggle is spiritual, and it encompasses our life from beginning to end. It attacks us from inside out, and from the outside in. As Chesterton says, we are living in a world that is not our own and yet for now, is our home. We might not be here forever, but right now, it's all we know. So, we must not only survive, but thrive as we discover what it means to battle on behalf of the Kingdom of God.

My friend John Bishop likes to ask people if they remember the verse: "I have come that they may have life, and have it …." He let's people fill in the last word, as you have done in your mind, saying aloud, "abundantly." And you are correct.

Did you catch that? The context of Jesus coming to give us life — and abundant life — is warfare...

This verse is John 10:10, and it promises a great truth. However, John Bishop then asks this question, "That's the second half of the verse. Can you tell me what the first half of that verse says?" You might be surprised to hear that the first half of the verse says: "The thief comes only to steal and kill and destroy." Did you catch that? The context of Jesus coming to give us life—and abundant life—is warfare: The devil is after everything that is precious to God; Satan seeks to steal, kill, and destroy what rightly belongs to God. And chief among His precious creation is us.

We must have a worldview that recognizes the warfare aspect of our calling. To find our place in God's story, we need to understand that Satan diametrically opposes this pursuit of finding our calling.

To handle the threat of living in such a hostile and dangerous place, we must know one fact: We did not get here first! Jesus beat us to this place—He went before us—and He is here with us. We are not alone. And in this one truth, we find a call to purpose and significance because ultimately we are not fighting our war. God is. I like the way C.S. Lewis describes it:

We live in enemy-occupied territory. That is what the world is. Christianity is the story of how the Rightful King has landed in disguise and is calling us all to take part in a great campaign of sabotage.[49]

So, as we hammer out an understanding of our part in God's great transcendent story, the outcome of this cosmic battle between good and evil is already determined. While God expects us—and commands us—to engage in warfare on behalf of His kingdom, we need to be certain that to the same degree life is fraught with danger and violence, it is also saturated with the grace, power, and reality of God's Kingdom. If we lose this context, we have lost our own personal battle to find significance, to live a holy life, and to find our calling.

We are called to the story of the "Rightful King," whose own campaign of sabotage invites us into His transcendent story, and whose outcome will be celebrated throughout eternity. And I have a role to play in that story, and so do you. We each play a role that is significant in direct proportion to the grace and love given to us by the Author and Creator of life itself. Your unique role has your name written all over it.

Satan opposes our calling through very specific strategies. The apostle Peter wrote that Satan prowls about like a "roaring lion, seeking whom he may devour" (1 Peter 5:8). Among the ways he "seeks to devour us" are deception, accusation, and confusion. He uses the arenas of money, sex, and power to get us to buy in to his lie, which the book of 1 John calls the lust of the eyes, the lust of the flesh, and the pride of life (see 1 John 2:16). However, God has wired the perfect antidote and protection from all of the devil's schemes into His design for our life in Christ.

One defense against Satan might surprise you: our weakness. Let's look at it more closely.

THE CHALLENGE OF WEAKNESS

One writer insightfully pointed out, "The place of our greatest vulnerability is the vacuum created between our need and God's provision."[50] However, when you are in the middle of a test or trial, it's nearly impossible to see God's shrewd plan on the move. In fact, as I look back at my own times of testing, I can see God's hand. But in the middle of those experiences I experience isolation. Intellectually, I understand that I'm not really isolated, but it's what I feel. I've sat with many friends while they are right in the middle of a life test, and I've felt much like one of Job's friends — with little to say, humbled, sobered by the weight of the trial. A son diagnosed with cancer, a wife whose heart has shut down toward the man of her youth, a friend whose fruitless year of searching for a job has left him crushed. We sit in silence, with nowhere to turn, nothing to say. In these dark times, our strength has left us, and we are acutely aware of our frailty and weakness.

Like you, in those heavy moments, I want to take away the source of the pain—even if only for a moment. But deep down, I know that the best course I can take is to help the other person hear the question. There is always a question that the trial asks—a deeper question of life that the struggle is trying to reveal. And God wants to reveal His truth through these experiences of testing and weakness.

In the epistle of James, we read about this process:

Consider it pure joy, my brothers, whenever you face trials of many kinds, because you know that the testing of your faith develops perseverance. Perseverance must finish its work so that you may be mature and complete, not lacking anything. If any of you lacks wisdom, he should ask God, who gives generously to all without finding fault, and it will be given to him. But when he asks, he must believe and not doubt, because he who doubts is like a wave of the sea, blown and tossed by the wind. That man should not think he will receive anything from the Lord; he is a double-minded man, unstable in all he does. (James 1:2-7).

If you haven't yet experienced a season of trials—deep and humbling ones that shake your optimism to the bone and your confidence to the marrow—then read this chapter with both eyes wide open before you step into your next assignment. Because here's the truth—the closer you get to the center of your calling, the hotter the trials in your life will be. When you go through the trials and testing, just remember this: The trials make you real. Get that? It's not your calling, your contribution, or your good ideas. It's you. The trials test you and call out perseverance in you.

Think about it. Who are you naturally drawn to? We seek out the person who has paid the price in battle and who has worked through the times of weakness and failure. These hard times bring about a kind of "authenticating." Undoubtedly, part of your calling and mission will grow out of the times of weakness that authenticate you. We see it in 2 Corinthians 1:3-4:

> *Blessed be the God and Father of our Lord Jesus Christ, the Father of mercies and God of all comfort, who comforts us in all our tribulation, that we may be able to comfort those who are in any trouble, with the comfort with which we ourselves are comforted by God.*

We are qualified to minister through the suffering we experience. We comfort others in the same ways with which we have been comforted. You remember Lorenzo Brown from earlier in the book—the man Don calls Jesus in a wheelchair. Lorenzo lives out these verses, ministering powerfully because he has persevered through some of the darkest trials imaginable, and he has received comfort from God.

Because our trials have the power to either delay or authenticate our calling, we must face certain questions. If we can answer these questions in a right and healthy way, we establish a foundation that makes us strong for the rest of our lives. Some of these questions include:

- Am I qualified to fulfill God's calling in my life?
- Is God really for me—and do I experience this truth in my life?
- What is God up to in my life?
- What is He teaching me through the trials I am facing?
- Am I experiencing these trials because I've done something wrong? Is He punishing me for mistakes I've made?

These questions and others like them uncover our motivations, fears, hopes, dreams, and desires. The answers to these questions become "interpreters" that help us understand what our lives mean. Weakness drives home the reality that we are fully and wholly dependent on God for our success. This realization shapes us to be humble before God and others.

The apostle Paul describes his own experience of God's transforming power. The experience was so mysterious and wrenching that Paul doesn't seem to be able to talk about it directly. So in the passage he talks about himself in third person:

> *I know a man in Christ who fourteen years ago was caught up to the third heaven. Whether it was in the body or out of the body I do not know—God knows. And I know that this man—whether in the body or apart from the body I do not know, but God knows—was caught up to paradise and heard inexpressible things, things that no one is permitted to tell"* (2 Corinthians 12:2-4).

The apostle explains that he was plagued by a "thorn"—an unspecified problem, obstacle, or hindrance that caused him great anguish. God didn't remove this thorn at Paul's request, and Paul came to view its persistence as a way of keeping him humble. Paul powerfully describes the relationship between weakness, struggle, the grace of God, and humility:

> *Therefore, in order to keep me from becoming conceited, I was given a thorn in my flesh, a messenger of Satan, to torment me. Three times I pleaded with the Lord to take it away from me. But he said to me, 'My grace is sufficient for you, for my power is made perfect in weakness.' Therefore I will boast all the more gladly about my weaknesses, so that Christ's power may rest on me. That is why, for Christ's sake, I delight in weaknesses, in insults, in hardships, in persecutions, in difficulties. For when I am weak, then I am strong"* (2 Corinthians 12:7-10).

In God's story, weakness is an opportunity—we might think of it as a pathway—to intimacy with God as we experience His grace. I am challenged by Paul's words, "For Christ's sake, I delight in weaknesses." A Kingdom secret is wrapped up in these verses, and we are wise to seek God for this truth to become reality in our lives.

DEALING WITH FAILURE

Of course, failure is different than weakness. But it also offers us an opportunity to grow in our pursuit of our calling and life mission.

When it comes to failure, Kyle Brotzman isn't a name you'd remember. I wouldn't have, except for his miscue in the fall of 2010. As the senior kicker and record holder for most points scored in a career, Kyle had a storied college football career for the Boise State Mustangs. The team was 11-0 going into the final week of the regular season. A win in their final game would have given them an outside shot at playing in the national title game, worth $12 million to the school making it onto this prestigious national stage. But first, Boise State had to get past 18th-ranked Nevada.

After a back-and-forth battle, with the game tied and just seconds remaining, the Boise State quarterback heaved a long towering pass that somehow, almost miraculously, came down into the arms of a Boise State receiver. Quickly signaling timeout and stopping the clock with just two seconds remaining, the Mustangs sent their place kicker, Kyle Brotzman, out for what appeared to be an easy chip shot to win the game—a routine 20-yard field goal, similar in length to an extra point.

You guessed it. The unbelievable happened—Brotzman missed. To make matters worse, Brotzman missed another chip shot in overtime, and minutes later, the Nevada kicker sealed the win.

Later that week, I heard an interview where Brotzman described the disappointment and frustration he experienced. Tens of thousands of kicks over years of practices and games. Yet, on this day he missed. A bigger challenge will present itself in the months and years ahead. It may wake him up in the middle of the night. It will creep into his thoughts in unguarded moments during the day. It will shuffle around the edges of his consciousness while he talks with a friend or listens to a professor's lecture. He'll replay the moment probably a thousand times, reaching for some other outcome, analyzing the kick over and over. Yet at the end of this process, nothing he can do will change the outcome.

Failure is like that. Undoubtedly all of us have our own versions of Kyle's story. Likely yours didn't occur on a national stage, but I bet your story gets messy at times, too. Failure is one of the inevitable consequences of living in this life. You weren't sure how it happened. You woke up one day, and you lost your job. Or your business went under. Or you realized that you hadn't been the dad you were called to be. Perhaps your failure came without any surprise—bad decisions you'd made for a long time "came to roost," and then you had to pay a price. A divorce. A problem with the law. A series of broken relationships. Even circumstances that might have been out of your control.

Like Kyle Brotzman, we all have opportunities before us to use failure as a chance to grow strong. In the days ahead, Kyle will have to make a choice: "Will I let this failure define me, or will I use it to become a better, stronger, wiser version of me?" You and I have the same choice before us: "Will I let this failure define me, or will I use it to become a better, stronger, wiser version of me?"

Of course, football is just a metaphor here. In the grand scheme of life, not important. But during these confusing, disorienting, and frustrating times, the wonderful truth that we must hold on to is this: *God is sovereign over every moment of our lives.*

In fact, let me go one step further. These times of failure are vital seasons of preparation that qualify us in ways that we can't plan for or practice ourselves. These deserts develop our calling. These times of failure and abject dejection are where we find out what's really real. The wise man or woman discovers the truth that "affliction is a treasure," as John Donne said, "and scarce any man hath enough of it."

We can easily underestimate both the risk and potential of failure. The same event can lead to defeat or greater victories, depending on how we deal with the circumstance. Edwin Markham's poem expresses this opportunity that trials offer:

> *Defeat may serve as well as victory*
> *To shake the soul and let the glory out.*
> *When the great oak is straining in the wind,*
> *The boughs drink in new beauty,*
> *And the trunk sends down a deeper root*
> *On the windward side.*
> *Only the soul that knows the mighty grief*
> *Can know the mighty rapture.*
> *Sorrows come to stretch out spaces*
> *In the heart for joy.*[51]

Tough times lead to the capacity for joy. This Kingdom reality of turning hard things into precious things can really make us distinctive. If you're not paying attention, you might completely miss the promise of Jeremiah 30:18: "I will restore the fortunes of Jacob's tents and have compassion on his dwellings; the city will be rebuilt on her ruins, and the palace will stand in its proper place." God's promise comes at the low point in Israel's life as a nation. God is making a beautiful promise to Israel—and I believe He makes the same promise to you and me.

When I traveled in Europe as a newly graduated college student, I remember coming upon fields where the flat land rose up in the shape of a mound, often a grassy knoll. No buildings were in sight on the otherwise flat plain. I learned that often these were the sites of towns hundreds of years earlier. They were mounds because each time a city experienced a devastating event—a fire, a defeat in war, or an abandonment of the town—a new city would be built on the rubble of the previous city.

When God promises that a city will be built on the ruins, He is promising to build on our failures. A palace will stand where a pile of rubble previously lay in ruins. God's work will arise from the messes of our lives. God fulfills this truth in the Messianic promises of Isaiah 61, and Jesus echoes the promise in Luke 4: good news, healed hearts, freedom, comfort, favor, beauty, praise, uprightness, to name a few. Read these passages and meditate on what the Lord has already done through the coming of His Kingdom.

Even for people who have a track record of external success, we all experience internal battles—those failures that take place where no one sees—in the core of our identity. In our work with leaders, we've seen what Frederick Buechner refers to as "the other war" as the primary challenge for leaders. Buechner writes:

> *The other war is not to conquer but the war to become whole and at peace inside our skins. It is a war not of conquest now but of liberation because the object of this other war is to liberate that dimension of selfhood which has somehow become lost... This is the other war—to become a human being.*[52]

The other war is an internal battle for authenticity, the place of our true identity. Most leaders spend their lives trying to find who they are from the look of approval in others' eyes; they seek validation and assurance that they have what it takes. In fact, that's why struggling through failure is so powerful. Failure requires us to step back to evaluate the story we're living in, and then to take a careful and reflective look at who we are. Failure helps us go back to God to hear again who He says we are. In the midst of our calling—as we work it out every day of our lives—failures threaten the trajectory of our calling. But when we hear from God in the midst of these times, we are re-energized by *who we are and who God is.*

The experience of failure requires us to discern between the voice the Enemy (of doubt and condemnation) and the Voice of our Father (of affirmation and acceptance).

Most men and women who are living out their life's purpose are learning the discipline of humility, and so they are less likely to interpret every event or circumstance, passing statement or other action, as a personal comment on their life. Their ego has moved out of the center.

THE SECRET PATH OF WARFARE AND WEAKNESS

Every person who is "finishing well" in life will tell you a little secret about warfare and weakness: that these inevitable battles and challenging weaknesses lead you down the path of the Kingdom of God. I believe this is true because the story we find ourselves in is an epic battle between good and evil. The drama is played out on a planet where a jealous and holy God has staked his rightful claim, and through a campaign of transforming love, raises up His people to establish a Kingdom that will never end. I also believe that because God is shaping each of us into His wonderful image, this temporary hardship looks forward to a glorious future. Jesus spoke of this tension — between the "now" and the "not yet" — when He declared that the kingdom of God was at hand.

Peter, whose own character was greatly shaped by experiences of failure and disappointment, wrote from his own hard-wrought faith in God. Listen for his clear vision of the future and how these temporary trials look forward to that wonderful future reality:

> *[God] has caused us to be born again to a living hope through the resurrection of Jesus Christ from the dead, to an inheritance that is imperishable, undefiled, and unfading, kept in heaven for you, who by God's power are being guarded through faith for a*

salvation ready to be revealed in the last time. (1 Peter 1:3-5).

Now listen to Peter's encouragement in the next few verses to God's people—to you and me—about the profit these trials promise for all of us who prevail through them:

In this you rejoice, though now for a little while, if necessary, you have been grieved by various trials, so that the tested genuineness of your faith—more precious than gold that perishes though it is tested by fire—may be found to result in praise and glory and honor at the revelation of Jesus Christ. Though you have not seen him, you love him. Though you do not now see him, you believe in him and rejoice with joy that is inexpressible and filled with glory, obtaining the outcome of your faith, the salvation of your souls. (1 Peter 1:6-9)

Doesn't God's Word bring the purpose of our lives into amazingly clear focus? As we seek to know God's desire for our calling and life mission, and as we set our hearts to persevere through the inevitable trials and challenging weaknesses we encounter, we can be certain that what we do in this life matters. At the same time, we are also convinced God is preparing us for a greater glory about which we catch only the faintest hints. I love the way C.S. Lewis speaks about this vision of the now and the not yet:

These small and perishable bodies we now have were given to us as ponies are given to schoolboys. We must learn to manage: not that we may some day be free of horses altogether, but that some day we may ride bare-back, confident and rejoicing, those greater mounts, those winged, shining and world-shaking horses which perhaps even now expect us with impatience, pawing and snorting in the King's stables.[53]

God invites us to ride in this life with confidence and courage — through the battles and struggles ahead — so our lives reflect the might and glory of our Savior, looking forward to the glorious reality of heaven.

Near the beginning of this chapter, we said that when warfare and weakness face us, we can choose one of two pathways: truth or lie. May you gaze upon the character of Christ and experience the reality of His truth as you press on — through every barrier and obstacle — to know Him more deeply every day.

Print the S.O.L.O. Workbook

Log on to **www.210project.com** and print your S.O.L.O. Workbook. You will want to take this into your day of solitude as you continue reading the next chapter.

11

SECRET OF DISCIPLINES
YOUR DAY OF SOLITUDE

"It is not the mountain we conquer but ourselves."

—Sir Edmund Hillary

Daina is a woman who meets with undergraduate students attending the university in her town. She hosts a weekly dinner in her home on Monday nights. She gets to know these students, encourages them, and shares her life with them. After she experienced a day of solitude, she said:

Toward the close of our study, we were encouraged to spend a day of solitude with the Lord. Although He had been affirming to me that I was doing what He had called me to do, this day alone with Him was pivotal. This day He clearly brought all the pieces together and gave me an intentional plan. This was the time when all my study and prayer came into focus and God gave me the strategy for His call in this new season of my life.

Daina's experience illustrates what we hope you've been learning from *The 2:10 Project*—that God is speaking to you. Even for a person like Daina, who had a strong sense of what God called her to do, uninterrupted time with God gave her a focus that was both inspiring and strategic.

We want to help you plan a day of solitude. However, immediately, you should be aware that you'll need to face down some obstacles. Busyness, fear, and doubt are just a few of the enemies you will have to confront to accomplish your day of solitude. In his classic book, *Celebration of Discipline,* Richard Foster says, "Our fear of being alone drives us to noise and crowds."[54] As a result, many obstacles stand in the way of scheduling time alone with God. In *Lead Like Jesus,* Ken Blanchard explains:

Solitude is a countercultural and challenging behavior. It draws us into the very place from which so much of our efforts are designed to help us escape-being truly alone with God without an agenda. It is a rare and often unsettling feeling to stop doing and just be.

Yet as strange as it feels to actively seek opportunities to "cease striving" (Psalm 46:10 NASB), the result can be life changing.[55]

This challenge—to take one day to pray and listen to God—is a lot harder than it appears. Before we take on the obstacles of the day of solitude, let me share a story from Don's life that drives home the powerful impact of the day of solitude. I am including the narrative here in Don's words:

In my first couple of years as a new believer, I was eager to grow, doing everything I could to learn as much as I could. During that time, I attended a weekend retreat led by a man named Dan Dehaun. If you're like me, you've learned that God often intersects us at the most random places to teach us. One such time happened through a conversation I had with Dan. He challenged me over lunch that weekend to spend one day a month in solitude with the Lord to learn to hear His voice. So, soon after his challenge, I marched off to spend a day on top of a mountain to experience my first day of solitude. It would be at least eight hours in prayer. I committed to it and promised myself I would not leave early.

Before I go any further, you need to know about Mrs. Ward. Mrs. Ward was a sweet woman who taught "Word Power," a course I had to take as a sophomore in high school. I always did well on her quizzes because, well, to put it bluntly, I cheated. On my desk, as "quick reference," I would pencil out several definitions of words I was unsure of. I got an A in the class and was never caught.

So, to return to my story about my first day of solitude. I spent 30 minutes praying about everything I could think of. I got uncomfortable, and I began to panic a little: What in the world am I going to do for the next seven and a half hours? Still, I forged on, even if it was a struggle. The day started to take shape as I read the Psalms and prayed through each passage. At some point, I started to experience a peace that I couldn't describe. Then, I started to ask God about my sin: What do I need to confess? Was there anyone in my life I needed to go and ask for forgiveness?

Then the craziest thing happened. The memory of Mrs. Ward popped into my head immediately. It was too weird. Where did that come from? I knew right away the Lord was telling me to find her and ask forgiveness for cheating on every test I ever took from her.

I objected, No way, God, that's too weird. Is that really what You are saying to me?

I tried to dismiss the thought, but God wouldn't let me. It became like a splinter in my mind. So, finally I cut a deal with God: Lord, if I run into her I will do it. Otherwise, I won't have any way of knowing if this is really from You or some crazy idea that came from me. *As my day ended, I was fairly confident that I would never see Mrs. Ward again—at least that was my hope.*

Two months later, at Thanksgiving, I was home from school. I was at a bookstore in the mall, and to my great astonishment, I looked up and saw Mrs. Ward walk into the bookstore. I panicked, hiding behind a bookshelf and hoping she'd leave, fearing the worst outcome if I did confess my sin to Mrs. Ward! Would they take away my high school diploma? Would I be thrown out of college? My parents would kill me. *My mind raced.*

But then, finally, I yielded to God's voice and obeyed.

"Mrs. Ward, do you remember me? Don Ankenbrandt. I was one of your 10th-grade Word Power students."

She remembered, probably mostly because of how unusual my last name is.

I continued, "Several years after I took your course, I had something profound happen to me that has changed my life. I became a follower of Jesus Christ. You might think I'm crazy, but about two months ago I was on a day of solitude praying about things I'd done wrong, wanting to become totally honest with my life. For some reason, I sensed God telling me that if I ever saw you again I would ask you to forgive me. You see, I cheated on every test I ever took from you, and I want to apologize."

What happened next was completely unexpected. Mrs. Ward started to cry! Again, a wave of panic rushed over me as we stood in the bookstore, tears streaming down her face. She asked me if we could go get a lemonade at a nearby fast food restaurant to talk. So we did.

What neither of us was ready for that day was God's great ambush of both of us. This was His plan—where my learning to listen to His voice and her life situation collided.

She explained, "I prayed this morning for God to show me, somehow, that He is there and cares for me. If nothing happened, I wouldn't believe in Him." She continued by asking me questions about why I had decided to follow Jesus.

I explained it all to her—how two years earlier, on a Thursday night, March 17, 1978, at the Trail West Young Life camp, I sat looking up at more stars than I'd ever seen. That night, I started my relationship with God, the One Who created everything. I explained how I went "all in" that day and my life was transformed from death to life in a moment.

Then I asked Mrs. Ward if she wanted to become a follower of Jesus, and she said yes. We prayed right there in the mall restaurant. And that day, Mrs. Ward came to know Jesus Christ. God gave me a life-changing experience, too—learning that He wants to use me, including my sin, to redeem my own life and to help others understand His grace and redemption.

Interestingly, one year later on the same Saturday before Thanksgiving, I was in a Christian bookstore in Huntsville and in walked Mrs. Ward. As we hugged, a moment of sheer joy ensued for both of us. She went on to tell me what had transpired in her life since meeting Jesus. Her marriage had been transformed, her children had all come to Christ, and that day in particular she was in the Christian bookstore trying to find a new study to use in her quiet times. After our hour-long conversation, I got in my car and just cried in gratitude for God allowing me to see how powerful He is, and for beginning to learn how to listen to His voice.

That day back in 1980 convinced me that I need to continue to spend extended time alone each month with the Lord, to learn to listen to His voice. Over the years, I've learned that God doesn't scream at us. He whispers. And if we learn to listen, He welcomes us into a more intimate and meaningful relationship with Him. Over the past 30 years, I've tried to make it a habit to spend one day a month with Jesus. As I look back, I see that God has used these times alone with Him to shape my life. He has taught me more than I could ever imagine about Who He is and what His plans are for me.

Isn't that an amazing story? I love the beautiful way Don teaches us about God and His invitation to come away with Him so we can learn to hear His voice. And when we hear His voice, unimaginable things happen.

CHALLENGES TO YOUR DAY OF SOLITUDE

Actually *doing* your day of solitude is a lot harder than it might seem, but not for the reason you might think. Just showing up is the biggest challenge you'll face.

We are inundated with busyness and superficiality. Richard Foster calls this "the curse of our age." We run so fast, and distraction is our constant companion. Longer work days filled with email, smart phones, iPads, Facebook, Twitter, video games, and hundreds of cable channels keep us constantly busy, busy, busy. We don't know how to slow down. Consequently, many of us miss hearing God's voice, experienced most often in His whisper.

We also face practical challenges. Where should you spend a day of solitude? How do you get time off work or away from family commitments?

On top of all of this will be the mental gymnastics that often accompany any change in our lives:

You'll think, *well, no, other more "spiritual" people do these kinds of things.* Or, *I'm not sure I really know God well enough to spend a day praying.* Or, *What's going to be the outcome...is it worth it?* Or, maybe the question we all wrestle with at some time in our lives, the one that is way down deep: *Will God answer me when I pray?*

SOLITUDE: TRUTH CLAIMS

Your day of solitude helps you to put into practice other spiritual disciplines in your life, including worship, prayer, fasting, meditation, the study of God's Word, service, and listening to God's voice. These spiritual disciplines provide a path for us to deepen our relationship with God — to grow in wisdom and understanding through reflection and insight and to become more sensitive to what God cares about as we learn to love others.

The day of solitude brings us face-to-face with God, confronting the busyness and stress of life that threatens our intimacy with Him. Jesus provides an outstanding example. Maybe you remember a scene from the book of Mark (Mark 1:29-38). Wonderful things had happened as part of a great day of ministry: blind people received their sight, and broken bodies and wounded hearts were made whole. Jesus had preached marvelous truths about the Kingdom of God.

But then He was gone. People were looking for Him, many of them with very real needs. The disciples couldn't even find Jesus.

What a stunning thing we see here! Essentially, Jesus walked away from the needs. Why? Because it wasn't His assignment on that day or at that time. He had another appointment—on the side of the mountain praying to His Father in Heaven. God's Word challenges us: "But without faith it is impossible to please Him, for he who comes to God must believe that He is, and that He is a rewarder of those who diligently seek Him" (Hebrews 11:6, NKJV). The day of solitude is a way for us to diligently seek God.

Solitude brings us face-to-face with ourselves. The day of solitude helps us to achieve a Sabbath balance in our active and stress-filled days. God's design creates order in our lives. God's design leads to balance.

STRATEGIES: PRACTICAL HELP FOR YOUR DAY OF SOLITUDE

As you know by now from the online exercises you've completed, your 2:10 M.A.P. will give you the pathway for your time with God on your day of solitude. You'll have questions, activities, and readings to help you make your day exactly what you need. As you look through your 2:10 M.A.P. and plan your day of solitude, here are some important considerations:

Prepare. Remember, you have an Enemy who works to keep you busy, distracted, and discouraged, especially when you desire to listen to your Heavenly Father. Though formidable, the devil is a defeated foe, so your objective is to stay focused on God and what He is calling you to do.

Place. Find a secluded place, preferably not your home. You need a change in scenery. If the weather permits, have your day of solitude outside at a park or lake or other natural setting. Also, remember there is probably no "perfect place." Find the best option you can, and go with it.

Pray. Take walks to think and pray. You might consider listening to some music that inspires you and helps you to worship God. Be sure to journal your thoughts and prayers. Consider praying through the Psalms, reading a verse aloud, then praying it back to the Lord. This process will guide your thoughts and often provides an outline of what God is doing or saying.

Reflect. Learning to spend extended time with God takes time. While your first day of solitude might be difficult, remember that God directs your thoughts and prayers. As you reflect on your life, you'll sense God's voice and leading. Consider bringing along other books to read to vary how you use your time. Leave your phone and computer behind — you don't need them.

Commit. These days take commitment, so you must resolve to engage in your day of solitude. Relax and learn and don't set preconceived expectations — let God shape your time. Committing to this day means you're undertaking a marathon, not a sprint.

Finally, this is important to hear: *God is not hiding from you.* On the contrary, He longs for us to spend time with Him. This is a mystery we might only come to understand in eternity — God delights when we seek Him. At times, you might feel that God is hard to find, but this isn't true. When we were lost, God found us. God speaks to us through His Word, through creation, through other people, through the circumstances of our lives, and in many other ways. His desire is for us to seek Him, "while He may be found" (Isaiah 55:6). Your day of solitude is a beautiful dance, between God and His precious child. May you catch a vision for the wonder and delight of seeking God.

These days of solitude will likely become some of the richest, most life-giving days in your relationship with God. Look forward to the time to relax, read books, listen to music, take a nap, enjoy long walks, and journal your thoughts. As you make this a part of your life, you'll have the chance to reread your journals from weeks and months and even years earlier, and see how your journey with God is marked and mapped in vivid detail. You'll find that some of those days were hard, some were frustrating, and some were revolutionary.

But every one of those days belong to you and to God.

Don says, "All of these days have woven in me a much deeper trust in the Lord God of this Universe and a confidence that He is worthy of my trust. He is passionate about all of us—and He loves to be alone with us."

So, with that, sit down right now, mark a day on your calendar, and go! God will be there, and that's a promise!

Update and print My 2:10 M.A.P.

Now it is time to log on to **www.210project.com** and document the information you completed in your S.O.L.O. Workbook. Log on to **www.210project.com** now to complete this step.

12

CALLING AND LEGACY

"I know the power obedience has of making things easy which seem impossible."

— Teresa of Avila

Anatole France said, "What we leave behind is a part of ourselves; we must die to one life before we can enter another." In many ways, this notion sums up the invitation and promise of calling. The invitation is to enter into a way of living that places God and His priorities at the center of our lives. It is a promise because when we do live our lives with God and His purposes at the center, we experience eternal life. Jesus said, "And this is eternal life, that they may know You, the only true God, and Jesus Christ whom You have sent" (John 17:3). At the end of the day, our reward for fulfilling our calling is God Himself, a deep and intimate relationship with our Father, Friend, Savior, Lord and King.

As we conclude *The 2:10 Project*, Don, Frank and I find it difficult to express the hope and expectation we have for what lies ahead of you. We fully expect God to speak to you, and we fully expect you to hear His voice. We also know that you will experience for the first time, or experience anew, the glorious privilege of giving away your life for the sake of the King. So, along those lines, we want you to hear a few parting words of encouragement directly from each of us:

DON'S WORDS OF ENCOURAGEMENT

"Before my father went to be with the Lord in 2007, our last few conversations took on a very different level of intensity. He said things he wished he'd said years earlier, encouraged me, and affirmed that he was proud of me. His final words were precious and sacred.

In a very similar way, Jesus had this kind of conversation with His disciples before His ascension. Listen well to His last words to them—and to us:

> *All authority has been given to Me in heaven and on earth. Go therefore and make disciples of all the nations, baptizing them in the name of the Father, the Son, and the Holy Spirit, and teaching them to observe all that I have commanded you. And lo,*

I will be with you always, even until the end of the age (Matthew 28:18, NASB).

Notice, Jesus didn't say, "Go to church and sit in the pews and learn as much as you can about me." Instead, Jesus made a proclamation for action, not a statement of passivity. *The 2:10 Project* is a journey and a process that we pray has changed your mindset as to how you approach your life from here on out—a process that has made you a person of action.

As I've coached many people over the last few years, I've seen a theme arise, which is captured by the word "intentional." Intentional is all about being purposeful—living day-to-day life with a focus to fulfill God's great adventure that He has for you in serving and knowing Him.

Also, reflect and meditate on the truth that you have a Father in heaven Who longs for you to live this adventure. He invites you to journey deep into an intimate life of knowing Him more. You also have an Enemy who is real and who seeks to thwart your efforts. He strategizes to discourage you, infuse lies into your mind—the chief one being "I'm not worthy of being used by God."

Ephesians 6 tells us to be on guard. Though the Enemy's presence on earth is real, we are the victors. You don't need to try this alone—travel and labor with others who share a common vision and heart as you.

In the book *Abandonment to Divine Providence*, Jean Pierre DeCasaude talks about how most believers live in two worlds, the past and the future. The past events of your life can trap you in a world of disappointment, bitterness, and longing, as well as wrong beliefs about God that have developed over time. This leaves us wishing we'd done many things differently, and we live a life of regret. However, God allowed these events to happen, so His purpose is for you to learn from them. Importantly, these events don't disqualify you; in fact, the exact opposite is true. Our past sins and wounds are often God's great platform for His mission through you and me. This is how He redeems our lives.

Many of us also fear the future—of what lies ahead, afraid of failure, especially as it pertains to ministry. Remember, the future isn't yours, and you have no control over it, not even 10 minutes from now. All you have is the moment you are in right now. So do your best to follow Jesus and leave the rest up to Him. DeCasaude calls this the "Sacrament of the Present moment," and it gives us a worldview that says life is sacred and that we can find Jesus in the small everyday moments of life. In these moments, we learn to trust Him and to serve others by giving our lives away. Ministry is right here, right now.

In following Jesus, I've come to believe that God usually does the opposite of what makes sense. I call it "the law of spiritual opposites." For example, the world system tells us that in order to be great we need recognition, status, and power. However, Jesus tells us if we want to be great we need to wash feet, serve, and set ourselves last. The world system says to accumulate as much as you can to create security for yourself and only give out of abundance. Jesus says that for true security, you need to give freely and sacrificially. In the same way, your greatest failures become the platform for your ministry to others—an opposing notion to the "common sense" views of the world.

Our natural temptation will be to look only for the big "God work" to fulfill our mission. Instead, we should look for the simple first and God may lead us to the big. God intersects you in the lives of so many people—this is where much of your mission gets played out. Young Life taught me "to do what you love and take people with you." Ministry is relational, so it requires time and sacrifice. But God doesn't want it to be a chore or misery. It should bring you life, fill your soul, and lead you to many adventures as you see the all-powerful, miraculous God use you as a part of His plan. Our only responsibility is to be intentional and obedient when He drops assignments into our path.

Finally, I encourage you to leave a legacy for your life. My friend and mentor Lloyd Reeb, in his *Halftime* coaching, asks people to dream about their 80th birthday. Imagine that all of the people you love come to celebrate your life so you can hear what they say as they toast your life. What would you want to hear from them? Could your family and friends speak about your relentless pursuit of knowing God and how your life had been marked by service and influencing others for Christ? Did your children and spouse see you serve? Were you generous with your life, both in relationships and in giving of your resources? What decisions will you make today to assure that you'll leave this life with a deep sense of joy for the wonderful life God has allowed you to have?

So I encourage you — get on with making the right choices. Learn to listen to God, and experience the life He invites you into: "I came to give life and give it to the full" (John 10:10). My hope is that *The 2:10 Project* is in the process of unlocking your potential, forever changing how you choose to live the life God gives you. Join us on this great adventure in discovering your place in God's great story."

FRANK'S WORDS OF ENCOURAGEMENT

"'Then I heard the voice of the Lord saying, 'Whom shall I send? And who will go for us?' And I said, 'Here am I. Send me!'" (Isaiah 6:8).

If you're like me, you've known for some time that God wants to get you in His game. In the inner-most place of your heart, you know the truth about being personally called to accomplish a Kingdom assignment. For me, it seemed as if I'd been wrestling with this notion for a lifetime, but I couldn't quite piece together exactly what God wanted me to do. Let me encourage you to trust that God will make it happen for you just as He did for me.

My prayer is that through your own day of solitude, you'll clearly hear God's voice. In fact, my hope is that, like Don, Marc, and me, your day of solitude will become a habit that lasts a lifetime. Keep pushing forward to understand who God made you to be and to find the places where your passion intersects with practical action. Continue to seek out others who complement your mission as you intentionally make your way past obstacles that would keep you from beginning and continuing your mission.

Expect that God will make some changes in your life. As we mentioned earlier in the book, my journey began as God broke my heart for hurting cities and communities across the country. That's when He began to accomplish some significant transformational work inside of me. And it felt good! I discovered that walking in harmony with the plan God designed for me was like living in my sweet spot. Being on mission with brothers that "get me" and understand my assignment is a gift from the Lord that every believer should experience.

Marc, Don, and I share an occasional laugh among ourselves related to the roles we play in the fulfillment of our mission. Marc can eloquently explain the theology—the *why* behind the calling God has placed on each of our lives. Don has spent years developing the process—the *how* of mentoring others to discover their special place in God's story. And me? Well, I have a vision and passion for *where* we live out calling—in our culture and in our communities as we mobilize the Body of Christ to take back ground conceded to the Enemy.

Take notice of the milestones on your 2:10 M.A.P. that might highlight key directional changes in your life. Recognize and act on them. Look for the obvious as well as subtle intersections between God's story and your own. Understand that God uses life experiences to equip us. Perhaps, like me, you need to take a closer look at seasons in your life: times when you were most happy, when you felt like you'd reached bottom, when the only place to turn was toward God, or when a key relationship began or ended in your life. Likely,

God has been trying to tell you something. My journey required that I take a risk and start walking toward a place where I was open to the Lord's direction. You'll find that God has given you everything you need for the assignment(s) planned specifically for you.

Keep in mind that taking even the smallest steps can have an amazing impact. Few launch global ministries, but never underestimate God's ability to work through you. I've met people across the country who have actively responded to God's call on their life. And He has used their gifts, talents, and passions to change the world:

- My friend Kevin organizes prayer walks to develop personal relationships with families of gang members in Orange County, California.
- Dale works in Pulaski County, Kentucky, to create the Healthy Family Mentoring Program.
- Steve organized an addiction coalition in Birmingham, Alabama.
- Bill and his church started a skateboarding ministry to teens in Colorado Springs, Colorado.
- Javier develops the musical abilities of disabled people working at the Salvation Army in Fort Lauderdale, Florida.
- Michelle, in Atlanta, works with other women in her church to provide babysitting services for families who can't pay for childcare.
- Rose plays the piano for residents at a hospice facility in Philadelphia.

The list goes on and on of people who can sincerely say, "I was made for this!"

What will you do for God? Keep in mind that it's not about *what* you do. Rather, it's about being responsive to what He's calling you to do. I encourage you to stay in touch with us. Let us know how your own adventure plays out. Send us an email, a video clip, join one of our discussion forums, or leave us a post on Facebook. Your story will inspire others into action, and who knows—you just might connect with a person who wants to join you on your journey. May God bless you and your desire to be everything He wants you to be."

MARC'S WORDS OF ENCOURAGEMENT

In the past 10 years, a very practical notion about what it means to glorify God has had a profound impact on me. This notion is what I would like to leave you with as we conclude *The 2:10 Project.*

First, a definition. "Glory," I would suggest, is "the visible manifestation of God's invisible qualities." Consider that for a moment. When God told Moses that He would allow His glory to pass by him, God made the invisible visible. This quality is what Moses called the "glory of God," and what he believed would kill him if he looked directly upon it. When Jesus came, John 1:14 says, "The Word became flesh and made his dwelling among us. We have seen his *glory*, the glory of the one and only Son, who came from the Father, full of grace and truth." What was invisible about God, became visible in Jesus Christ. One more passage to drive the point home:

> *[Jesus] is the image of the invisible God, the firstborn over all creation. For by him all things were created: things in heaven and on earth, visible and invisible, whether thrones or powers or rulers or authorities; all things were created by him and for him…For God was pleased to have all his fullness dwell in him (Colossians 1:15-16, 19).*

Did you catch that? In Jesus, God's glory is shown forth—the invisible qualities of God became visible to us in the person of Jesus Christ. Isn't that amazing?

But here is how it applies in a practical way. Jesus commands us to glorify God with our lives. What, practically speaking, does it mean to "glorify God?" Let me give you the practical application that changed my life. To glorify God means "to make the invisible qualities of God visible to the world around us."

In other words, because we know God to be kind, we show kindness—making this invisible quality of God visible to others. Because we know God forgives us, we forgive others—making this invisible quality of God visible to others. Because we know God to be the champion of the outcast and broken-hearted, and because He came to us when we were outcasts from heaven and broken-hearted in our own sin, we love and care for others and champion their healing and wholeness—making this invisible quality of God visible to others.

I would even suggest that this is the only reason God has left us on the earth: *To make the Invisible God visible to a lost and hurting world.* To glorify God—what a wonderful invitation! We make the invisible God visible through the day-in and day-out events of our lives. Our actions serve as living pictures of the character and nature of our loving God.

So whether we do that in our vocation, our ministry, as a neighbor, or in our family, we try to live our lives so that those around us get to know our God—whom we love with our whole hearts, Who has loved us with His transforming, eternal love.

This is the legacy that we believe is at the heart of *The 2:10 Project*—a life of service, lived out through our unique calling, within God's transcendent story. When we do that, our generation will certainly be changed, as well as the generations that follow.

As we conclude our time together, I want to share with you four ways that we'll be praying for you (and for ourselves) in the weeks and months ahead:

- That God would help us accurately interpret the parable of our lives, so that we can live out our identity as His workmanship, established on His truth.
- That God would give us the courage to engage our lives as

a heroic journey, walking with Jesus into the very center of His purpose, to see lives transformed by God's power.

- That God would help us walk alongside the friends He's led us to and to recognize the people He's called us to serve.
- That God would help us discover our unique spiritual DNA: our life mission and the specific strategies to live it out.

We look forward to seeing you online—perhaps in person—in the days ahead. To God be the Glory!

Continue the experience and share your story

Now it is time to share your story and calling with others. Log on to **www.210project.com** and click "Share my Story".

ENDNOTES

1. The term, "design passage," is one I learned from Dr. Del Tackett in his biblical worldview teaching.

2. Tackett, D. (Director). (2006). *The Truth Project* [Motion picture]. United States: Focus on the Family.

3. Beuchner, F. (1973). *Wishful Thinking: A Theological ABC.* New York: Harper & Row. page 95

4. I am indebted to Rodney Cox of Ministry Insights for the notion of data, meaningful interactions leading to transformation.

5. Chambers, O. (2008). *My Utmost For His Highest.* Newburyport, MA: Discovery House Publishers. (Original work published 1927)

6. James, W. (1991). *The Varieties of Religious Experience.* New York: Triumph Books. (Original work published 1902) Page 24

7. Chambers, O. (2008). *My Utmost For His Highest.* Newburyport, MA: Discovery House Publishers. (Original work published 1927)

8. Jones, Alan W. *The Soul's Journey: Exploring the Spiritual Life with Dante as Guide.* San Francisco: Harper

9. Anton, Mike. "The Hard Life—Santa Ana Style." *Los Angeles Times Magazine.* 04 September 2004.

10. This statistic was quoted widely in our partnership with Operation UNITE, a non-profit organization in the Fifth Congressional District of Kentucky, fighting drug abuse through a three-pronged approach, law enforcement, treatment and education.

11. Saint-Exupéry, Antoine De. *Flight to Arras.* New York: Harcourt, Brace and World, 1942. Cambridge, MA: Cowley Publications, 2001. Print.

12. Eusebius, Of Caeserea, and Paul L. Maier. *Eusebius—the Church History: a New Translation with Commentary.* Grand Rapids, MI: Kregel Publications, 1999. Print.

13. Barnett, Matthew, and George Barna. *The Cause within You: Finding the One Great Thing You Were Created to Do in This World.* Carol Stream, IL: Barna, 2011. Print.

14. Meinrad, Of Einsiedeln. *Saint Meinrad Prayer Book.* St. Meinrad, IN: Abbey, 1995. Print.

15. Max Lucado, *The Christmas Candle,* 2006. Nashville: WestBow Press, a division of Thomas-Nelson, Inc. Print.

16. Guinness, Os. *The Call: Finding and Fulfilling the Central Purpose of Your Life.* Nashville, TN: W Pub. Group, 2003. Print.

17. *Frontline:* The Merchants of Cool. Airdate: February 29, 2001. Directed by Barak Goodman, written by Rachel Dretzin, Produced by Barak Goodman and Rachel Dretzin. Copyright 2001 WGBH Educational Foundation.

18. "Greenspan Admits 'Flaw' to Congress, Predicts More Economic Problems | Online NewsHour | October 23, 2008 | PBS." *PBS: Public Broadcasting Service.* Web. 28 Aug. 2011. <http://www.pbs.org/newshour/bb/business/july-dec08/crisishearing_10-23.html>.

19. John Adams, *'Argument in Defense of the Soldiers in the Boston Massacre Trials,'* December 1770. U.S. diplomat & politician (1735 - 1826).

20. Bailey, Pearl. *The Raw Pearl.* Harcourt, Brace, World, 1968. Print.

21. Lewis, C. S. *Mere Christianity: a Revised and Amplified Edition, with a New Introduction, of the Three Books, Broadcast Talks, Christian Behaviour, and Beyond Personality.* San Francisco: HarperSanFrancisco, 2001. Print.

22. David White, from *Songs for Coming Home* c1989 Many Rivers Press

23. Dictionary.com, "transcendent." Retrieved at dictionary.reference.com/browse/transcendent.

24. Lewis, C. S. *Mere Christianity: a Revised and Amplified Edition, with a New Introduction, of the Three Books, Broadcast Talks, Christian Behaviour, and Beyond Personality.* San Francisco: HarperSanFrancisco, 2001. Print.

25. Dillard, Annie *The Writing Life.* New York: HarperCollins Publishers, 1989.

26. Dictionary.com, "assets." retrieved at dictionary.reference.com/browse/assets.

27. This term, "glory," to describe the expression of God's handiwork through each of our lives, comes from my close friend and colleague, Gary Barkalow, author of *It's Your Call: What Are You Doing Here?, published by David C. Cook, 2010.*

28. Spirit-Filled Life Bible, Thomas-Nelson Publishers, Nashville, TN. Copyright 1991. Page 1831.

29. Strong's, #4678, Retrieved at www.studylight.org/isb/view.cgi?number=4678

30. Strong's #1108, Retrieve at www.studylight.org/isb/view.cgi?number=1108

31. Strong's #4102, Retrieved at www.studylight.org/isb/view.cgi?number=4102

32. Strong's #4394, Retrieved at www.studylight.org/isb/view.cgi?number=4394

33. Strong's #1100, Retrieved at www.studylight.org/isb/view.cgi?number=1100

34. See 1 Corinthians 14:1-4

35. Strong's #4166, Retrieved at www.studylight.org/isb/view.cgi?number=4166

36. Strong's #1320, Retrieved at www.studylight.org/isb/view.cgi?number=1320

37. For our purposes, a "truth claim" is a biblical concept or doctrine that says it alone is the truth and opposing opinions are false. In other words, Scripture proclaims a statement is true, so we are accepting that indeed it is the truth. Tackett, D. (Director). (2006). *The Truth Project* [Motion picture]. United States: Focus on the Family.

38. *Poems and Prose of Gerard Manley Hopkins* By Gerard Manley Hopkins, W. H. Gardner.

39. *Spanish Fly* TV with Jose Wejebe. Retrieved on September 1, 2011 at www.spanishflytv.com/article/reel-life-adventures-dominican-republic/.

40. Gardner, John, *Excellence: Can We Be Equal and Excellent Too?* New York: Norton and Company, 1987.

41. McManus, Erwin, *Uprising: A Revolution of the Soul*, Nashville: Thomas Nelson Publishers, 2006, p. 8.

42. Chambers, O. (2008). *My Utmost For His Highest*. Newburyport, MA: Discovery House Publishers. (Original work published 1927).

43. McManus, Erwin, *Uprising: A Revolution of the Soul*, Nashville: Thomas Nelson Publishers, 2006, p. 9.

44. Dictionary.com, "mission." Retrieved at dictionary.reference.com/browse/mission

45. Dictionary.com, "mission." Retrieved at dictionary.reference.com/browse/mission

46. Henri Nouwen, *Gracias!* (New York: Harper Collins, 1983), pp 147-148.

47. *The Broadview Anthology of Seventeenth Century Verse & Prose,* Alan Rudrun (editor), Joseph Black (editor), and Holly Faith Nelson (editor), (Peterborough, Ontario: Broadview Press, Ltd., 2000).

48. Chesterton, G. K., *Orthodoxy,* Copyright 1908 John Lane Company, Reprinted in 1995 by St. Ignatius Press, San Francisco.

49. Lewis, C. S. *Mere Christianity: a Revised and Amplified Edition, with a New Introduction, of the Three Books, Broadcast Talks, Christian Behaviour, and Beyond Personality.* San Francisco: HarperSanFrancisco, 2001. Print.

50. McManus, Erwin, *Stand Against the Wind: Awaken the Hero Within* (Nashville: Thomas Nelson Publishers, 2006), Kindle Location 535.

51. *Contemporary Verse: New Ed (Granger Index Reprint Series),* Grace E.W. Sprague (author, editor), A. Marion Merrill (author, editor). (p.24)

52. Buechner, Frederick. *Listening to Your Life,* New York: Harper Collins, 1992, p. 244.

53. Lewis, C.S., *Miracles,* New York: HarperCollins, 1974, p. 299.

54. Foster, Richard, *Celebration of Discipline.* New York: HarperCollins Publishers p. 96.

55. Ken Blanchard and Phil Hodges, *Lead Like Jesus,* (Nashville: Thomas Nelson Publisher, 2005), p. 155.